The Essence of
FEMINISM

The Essence of
FEMINISM
THE MODERN BELIEFS SERIES

Kirsten Birkett

❀ MATTHIAS MEDIA

The Essence of Feminism
© Matthias Media, 2000

St Matthias Press Ltd ABN 19 067 558 365

PO Box 225, Kingsford NSW 2032, Australia
Telephone: (02) 9663 1478   Facsimile: (02) 9662 4289
International: +61-2-9663 1478   Facsimile: +61-2-9662 4289
Email: sales@matthiasmedia.com.au
Internet: http://www.matthiasmedia.com.au

Distributor in South Africa:
Christian Book Discounters

Suite 221, Postnet X 18, Rondebosch 7701
Ph: (021) 685 3663
Email: <peter@christianbooks.co.za>

Unless otherwise indicated, Scripture verses taken from:
the HOLY BIBLE, NEW INTERNATIONAL VERSION.
Copyright ©1973, 1978, 1984 International Bible Society.
Used by permission of Zondervan Bible Publishers.

ISBN 1 876326 25 5

Cover design and typesetting by Joy Lankshear Design Pty Ltd.
Printed in Australia.

Contents

Preface

THE MODERN BELIEFS SERIES

The world is shaped by what we believe: our values, our society, our daily activities will reflect what we believe to be true and important. This is the case for everyone, not just those who consider themselves 'religious' or 'having faith'. Whatever beliefs a person may hold, be they secular, atheist, religious, modern, traditional, scientific, artistic or a mixture of them all, that person's world view and way of life will reflect the underlying ideological conviction.

Most people go through life happily (or unhappily) unaware of their beliefs. It's easy to assume that what we think is what everyone does, or just never think about it at all. It's a sad way to be, both for individuals and for the society we create. If Socrates considered "the unexamined life is not worth living", we might add "the unexamined society is not worth having"—if we don't understand what we believe and why society is the way it is, we will never be able to affect it for the better.

The 'Modern Beliefs' series is not meant to be the final word on everything. It is meant to describe the essence of the beliefs that pervade our world; the ideas that tell us who we are, why we are here and what we ought to do about it. There are many such ideas, most of them inherited from past ages, some newly invented. We have no particular criteria for what comes under the heading 'Modern Beliefs'; if it has affected our culture today, it's worth understanding.

Our world is full of so many ideas it can be confusing just waking up in the morning. We hope that the 'Modern Beliefs' series will help to make at least a few parts of it more understandable.

About *The Essence of Feminism*

I began this book as a feminist, in my conscious labelling of myself as well as in my basic assumptions about men and women. I have thought of myself as a feminist throughout my adult life, and have read and approved, as well as critiqued, a wide range of feminist texts. It seemed a basically sensible philosophy. Women deserve to be treated with exactly the dignity and respect that men do as human beings. I grew up with this attitude, was always encouraged to plan my future as I wished, and was offered the opportunity for education and career on precisely the same grounds as my brothers. I have completed two university degrees and am working on a third; I have received recognition for my work; I have financial independence, a career, a satisfying social life and good relationships with my colleagues, both male and female. I value my freedom and my life achievements. In all this, I felt gratitude to the movement which created a world in which I could live this way.

Some years ago I became a Christian, and my thought was to write a book about the interaction between Christianity and feminism. Both philosophies promote justice and human rights, and although there are some differences, I felt sure that the result would be a recognition of the value of women and the strengths of feminism, within a Christian framework.

I started by trying to gain a firm grasp of feminism—its origins, its history and development, its basic philosophy and view of the world, its achievements and consequences. Having done so, I planned to explain how it related to Christian thought, and what insights biblical Christianity might bring to bear on the subject.

I did not get that far. What I found as I immersed myself in feminist literature and history was not at all what I had expected. It quite revolutionized my thinking. As it turned out, this part of the research expanded to fill the entire book. This is no longer a book about Christianity and feminism; in fact, I barely mention Christianity until almost the last page (which may be a relief to some readers and a disappointment for others).

This book is about feminism: what it is, how it developed, and what changes and consequences it has wrought in Western society. It is not the answer for every problem women face in society. Questions of how a woman should organize her life, whether she should go to university, marry, work, have children or none of these, are still questions that a woman must work out for herself. What this book argues is that whatever she decides, she should not look to feminism for the answers. By its end, I hope that readers will understand why, having begun my research as a feminist, by the end I was one no longer.

Kirsten Birkett
SYDNEY, 2000

Chapter 1

THE PROBLEM WITH MANY NAMES

In 1877, Charlotte Elizabeth McNeilly attempted to gain a divorce from her husband of twenty-six years. She recounted in detail the violence her husband had committed; he had threatened to murder her, chased her with a meat fork, left her body bruised black by kicks, nearly choked her, and pushed a stick down her child's throat (the child later died). She had evidence of her husband's adultery, too. She had tried to earn her own living apart from him but he had confiscated her earnings, which under law he was entitled to do. Her petition for divorce was unsuccessful; the judge was unconvinced she had established her case, and it was dismissed with costs.[1]

Charlotte McNeilly suffered terribly. Her story is told in the introduction to a recent book on feminism, in order to demonstrate the injustices that women of the past suffered, which feminism tried to right. It is the kind of story used in arguing that reform of divorce laws, for example, was badly needed by the end of the nineteenth century. Feminists fought for such reform, so that cases such as Charlotte McNeilly's need never happen again.

What is the lot of women today, more than 120 years later? After decades of vigorous feminist lobbying and considerable change in both laws and social attitudes regarding women, how are women faring? One would expect the picture to be far happier. With such a strong movement, which has been so influential, women ought to be far better off than they were in Charlotte McNeilly's day.

It seems paradoxical, then, the lot of women in society today is not at all happy. Domestic violence against women is at record levels, and women generally fear to walk alone at night. Teenage

---

1   Marylin Lake, *Getting Equal: The History of Australian Feminism*, Allen and Unwin, Sydney, 1999, pp. 2-3.

girls starve themselves to fit an artificial, unhealthy definition of beauty, while belittling images and anti-women lyrics fill rock songs. Mothers struggle in poverty to care for their children, or bear the double burden of paid work and housework.

These problems seem to revolve around two issues in particular: marriage and work. In both areas, women are disadvantaged and suffering. Anecdotal evidence of this is found in just about every newspaper or social magazine; complaints about tiredness, stress, too much work, coping with housework and looking after children while chasing a career, and worrying about the divorce or the next relationship in the meantime. The conflicting calls of work, financial independence, fulfilment, mortgage, children, love and romance—as teenage angst, twenty-something confusion or thirty-plus separations—are now the basis of the most popular sitcoms and dramas on television. Women have never been stronger, these stories proclaim, have never had so many advantages—so why is life so impossible to live?

There's a new breed of family in Australia. Open any newspaper and you'll see them. The football hero proudly nursing his newborn baby. Beside him is his partner, the child's mother. At the opening of a new kindergarten, there's a young de facto couple playing with their cute toddler. Cohabiting parents are so commonplace that their unmarried status no longer attracts comment.

(SYDNEY MORNING HERALD, 2/12/99)

In this chapter, we will explore some of the realities of modern life for women. Marriage has changed: it is no longer the only basis for romantic relationships, and is no longer a lifelong commitment that is dauntingly hard to leave. Work for women has changed: the place of a mother is no longer in the home, and the popular image of a mother has changed from housewife to the power-suited woman dropping the kids at childcare on the way to the office. Although we are told that these changes are indisputably for the good, that they represent the progress of justice and enlightened civilisation of the highest order, the actual statistics about women's lives fail to match the rhetoric.

THE DECLINE AND FALL OF MARRIAGE

Over the past several years, the social norms governing relationships have changed dramatically. Marriage has been redefined, downgraded and made much easier to break. Divorce has become far more prevalent in the last twenty-five years. When the no-fault Family Law Act was introduced in 1976, there was a sudden, major increase in the number of divorces (63,230 in 1976 compared to about 9,000 per year in the decade 1961-70). The number has remained far above pre-1976 days ever since. It is estimated that now 43% of marriages will fail.[2] While Australia cannot yet match the divorce rate of the US, it is fifth in line after Sweden, England and Canada.

What we must come to terms with is how bad this trend has been. This is an unpopular view, to be sure—public comment is generally rather snide about those who would lament the breakdown in marriage. Yet study after study is demonstrating that the increase in divorce is bad for people—bad for women, bad for men and especially bad for children. As the shackles of marriage have loosened, many women have unfortunately not found freedom from anything except security and economic

---

2   *To Have and to Hold: a report of the inquiry into aspects of family services,* House of Representatives Standing Committee on Legal and Constitutional Affairs, Canberra, 1998, pp. 15-16. This report surveys hundreds of studies and submissions from research institutes on marriage and related issues, and draws together their results. It is freely available from Parliament House, Canberra.

comfort.[3] Marriage, unpopular and dated as its image is, is actually very good for women. Its recent decline has had, consequently, rather terrible results for women and their children.

The Inquiry into Youth Homelessness has identified family breakdown as a major cause of thousands of children leaving home.[4] Children of divorced parents tend to have poorer marriages themselves and a greater likelihood of divorce. They are much more susceptible to psychiatric illness, excessive drinking, asthma and injury. Both boys and girls suffer increased behavioural problems and delinquency. Divorce affects youth depression and suicide, and girls' sexual permissiveness—which is again directly correlated to the likeliness of future divorce. Children of divorce are less likely to attend university and be employed.[5]

These conclusions are not anecdotal generalisations; they derive from extensive and repeated research. What is more, they come from studies that are adjusted for socio-economic levels. That is, it is not just that children of divorce are likely to suffer a lower standard of living, perhaps moving house and schools, and so on. While this is true, it is not the only cause of their educational and social problems. Over and above such factors, divorce affects children adversely. There is even evidence to indicate that the accepted wisdom that it is better to end a high conflict

---

3   It is often assumed that the increase in divorce has the positive side of releasing women from violent or abusive marriages. However the numbers of divorces in which physical violence is given as the reason are low—a recent Australian study puts it at 6%. See Ilene Wolcott and Jody Hughes, 'Towards understanding the reasons for divorce', Australian Institute of Family Studies Working Paper 20, June 1999, p. 9.

4   Human Rights and Equal Opportunity Commission (1989) *Our Homeless Children* Canberra, AGPS, quoted in *To Have and to Hold*, p. 19.

5   These conclusions are drawn from nearly thirty separate studies of data from America, England and Australia, cited in *To Have and to Hold*, pp. 35-37. Nonetheless, contrary views still promote controversy as individual researchers claim divorce has no bad effects on children, such as reported in the story 'Divorce not all bad news for children', *The Sydney Morning Herald*, 26/7/00.

marriage 'for the sake of the children' than to continue it, is a misunderstanding of the reality.[6]

It is not just children who suffer—divorce is bad for everyone. For both men and women, marriage is the best protector against illness and premature death.[7] Married women live longer and are less likely to have cancer than single women. Marriage breakdown is one of the biggest causes of suicide and depression. On just about any indicator, if you want to stay healthy, you should get (and stay) married.

We are probably all familiar with the difficulties that divorced mothers face, especially economically. Julia Truss, of Sylvania, chose to give up her career as a graphic designer when her children were born. Now, after her divorce, she works 9.15 to 2.45pm five days a week, earning $220 net, and receives a sole parent payment of $95 a week, as well as the Family Allowance of $125 a week.[8] Separation and divorce continue to put such women into poverty in Australia. Single parents are among the poorest groups in the community, and around 86% are female.[9] There has been a substantial increase in single parent families in Australian society, whether through divorce or never marrying. In June 1999, 15% of all families were one parent families.[10] Figures from 1986 showed that while only 2.4% of couples with one child were in severe poverty (defined as having an income below 80% of the poverty line), 14.2% of sole parents with one child were in that category. 13.6% of couples with one child were in the next category—living *near* poverty—compared to

---

6 Based on a British study, 1994. *To Have and to Hold*, p. 43.
7 Based on a 1997 literature review. *To Have and to Hold*, p. 27.
8 *The Sydney Morning Herald*, 13/12/99.
9 'Labour force status and other characteristics of families, Australia, June 1999', ABS [Australian Bureau of Statistics] no. 6224.0
10 *Ibid.*

58.1% of sole parents with one child.[11]
The consequences of divorce also extend beyond the immediate families. Research into the relationships between generations also shows the effects of divorce. If parents of young children divorce, they are not only likely to have a weaker relationship with their children, but also with grandchildren when they arrive. If parents of adult children divorce, this can also weaken grandparent-grandchild interaction. Also, where adult children have no partner, it is more likely that grandparents will never see their grandchildren.[12]

There are more subtle effects that contribute to the misery of separated parents. Only 3% of children in single-parent families have their other parent sharing their care. This is despite the fact that divorced parents all give strong assent to the proposition that both parents share responsibility for the care, contact and financial supports of children—non-resident fathers being the strongest supporters of this ideal. Indeed 95-98% of Australians, whether divorced or not, agree that parents have responsibility to give children love and emotional support, to teach them right and wrong, and to look after their education. This suggests that the hundreds of thousands of non-resident parents do not live up to their own requirements for parenting. They have to live with the fact that they do not, or cannot, care for their children as they

---

11 'Australia now—a statistical profile: income and welfare, special article—poverty and deprivation in Australia', Australian Bureau of Statistics, 1996. Neither is the poverty of divorced mothers just a result of unfair settlement laws, as the popular impression is. Having sole custody of children, which divorced mothers frequently do, can even attract more money at settlement. Whether settlement is fair or not is difficult to assess, and men and women's feelings about whether the outcome of their divorce was fair are roughly the same. See Wolcott and Hughes, *op. cit.*, p. 18.

12 However, most grandparents still endeavoured to see their grandchildren, mostly children of daughters. Christine Millward, 'Aspects of grandparenting', Australian Institute of Family Studies, 1996.

would like to. This is a misery with little hope for resolution.[13]

Yet perhaps this just means that patterns of relationships ought to change. Perhaps marriage itself is being approached wrongly, and other ways of establishing permanent relationships ought to be tried—such as living together first, without jumping into a pressured commitment such as marriage.

According to the Australian Bureau of Statistics, 67% of couples marrying in 1998 had cohabited prior to marriage, compared to 22% in 1978.[14] De facto relationships have increased not only in number, but in public approval. In one 1995 survey, 55% of people agreed that a 'trial' marriage was appropriate preparation for a real one. A large majority agree that it is all right for a couple to live together without planning to marry. This reflects a view that has been dominant since the seventies; that living together before marriage is the best way to ensure that marriage is successful.[15] It's a view that still holds. "[Marriage] is breathtakingly romantic", writes journalist Adele Horin, "and from the perspective of the 21st century, totally crazy... Young couples today are less able to take such a leap of faith, and who can blame them?... Now commonsense plays a bigger role in setting up, and it should."[16] After all, surely having a 'practice' marriage first is a sensible preparation for a life-long commitment?

Unfortunately, that has not proved to be true. According to the Australian Institute of Family Studies, after five years of

13 Kate Funder, 'We hold these truths: a national perspective on parental responsibility', Australian Institute of Family Studies, 1996; 'Family Characteristics, Australia, 1997', ABS no 4442.0.
14 'Marriages and divorces, Australia', 1998, ABS no 3310.0.
15 Conclusions drawn from some six separate studies on cohabitation, in *To Have and to Hold*, pp. 76-78.
16 *The Sydney Morning Herald*, 17/6/00.

marriage, 13% of those who had cohabited before marriage would divorce, compared to 6% of those who had not. Twenty years later, 56% of those who cohabited before marriage would have divorced, compared to 27% of those who had not.[17] These trends have been found in numerous studies throughout the Western world. If you live together before marriage, you are far more likely to end up divorced. It is one of the strongest correlating factors. Rather than being a 'trial' marriage which will ensure a better result, living together seems to be particularly bad for marriage. Even those who do not divorce score significantly lower on measures of quality of marriage. Couples who live together before marriage have significantly lower scores in both perceived quality of marital communication and marital satisfaction.[18]

That is not the only way in which de facto couples suffer. The rate of violence is appreciably higher for cohabiting couples than for married couples. Children of de facto couples are also severely disadvantaged. Across a range of life issues, they perform at lower levels than children of married couples. At school, in sport, in social skills; in the level of education achieved, in employment, in drug use, and in crime and delinquency, children of cohabiting couples are far more likely than children of married couples to be at the bad end of the scale.[19] Serial de facto relationships are even worse. A child whose mother lives with a man other than the child's father is at least five times more likely to be abused than one who lives with both married parents. The proportion of suspected killers in de facto relationships is 6.5 times higher than for the general population.[20]

---

17 This matches research in Canada, the US and the UK. *To Have and to Hold*, p. 79.
18 *Ibid.*, pp. 81-82.
19 Results of studies 1996-1998. *To Have and to Hold*, pp. 82-83.
20 Data from the Australian Institute of Health and Welfare, the National Children's Bureau of Australia and other studies. *To Have and to Hold*, p. 47.

In short, the extensive data that is now available points to only one conclusion—that the collapse of marriage during the last quarter of the twentieth century has been a disaster for women, economically, socially, parentally and personally.

However, even women with intact marriages do not seem to be very happy. This brings us to the second major problem we can identify for women today: work.

WORK

A recent newspaper article on women and work included these comments:

> *'Feminism has saved capitalism' US communitarian Philip Selznick said in a Melbourne lecture. His point was not about feminism, which he supported as opening women's lives to opportunities of paid work, but about contemporary capitalism. Feminist emphasis on paid work for women, he argued, has been used to deflect attention from the unpalatable fact that so many families now need two adult earners just to maintain living standards.[21]*

In families with dependents, 60% of wives are now employed, with a steady rise since the early 1980s of the number of wives in full-time employment.[22] Roughly equal proportions of men and women who are employed have dependent children; 39% of men and 38% of women.[23] Broken up according to the age of the youngest child, the figures are even stronger. 48% of wives with youngest child under five are in the workforce. When the

---

21 *The Weekend Australian*, 20-21/11/99
22 Ilene Wolcott and Helen Glezer, *Work and Family Life: Achieving Integration*, Australian Institute of Family Studies, 1995, p. 9.
23 *Ibid*; figures are for 1994.

youngest child is 5-9 years, the percentage increases to 67%; and amongst wives whose youngest child is 10-14, 72% are employed. The numbers of these women working full-time shows a similar pattern. Of wives with a child under five, 34% work full-time; 40% of those with children 5-9 are employed full-time; and 50% of married mothers with teenage children are employed full-time. For single mothers, the respective percentages are even higher.[24]

The structure of the workforce has certainly changed since 1961, when only 17% of married women aged 25-34 were in the labour force. Various factors made this change possible. Shifting patterns of urbanization and labour-saving domestic appliances have changed the nature of householding. Legislation concerning maternity leave and equal-opportunity employment has made it easier for women to get jobs. There has been considerable expansion in the recreation, personal and services sectors in which women are likely to work; at the same time, job losses have mainly been in blue collar industries such as manufacturing, construction and mining, which were more generally male. All such factors meant that if women wished to work, they had considerably more opportunity to do so.

These changes made it possible for women to work, but do not explain why so many women have taken up the opportunity. Part of the story has been the increase of numbers of women with university degrees since the expansion of universities (and introduction of free tuition) in the 60s. Moreover, universities themselves have become more oriented towards vocation—training for a particular career—than general education. Not only are more women tertiary-educated, but they are educated in courses which lead naturally to expectations of a career —law, medicine, social work, accounting and so on.

---

24 *Ibid.*, pp. 10-11. More detailed breakdowns of figures are also available in this book.

More generally, however, the reasons have been largely economic. Since the Second World War, there has been a steady fall in real wages for middle and lower income workers, loss of employment at middle level for adult males due to economic recession and industrial restructuring, new standards of consumption, and increasing costs of housing.[25] Many families need more than one income. Amongst mothers who decide to work part-time rather than full-time, 82% do so to look after their children even though only 44% earn enough income that way. Staying home to look after children, although the preferred option for most mothers, means economic hardship. By far the majority of mothers feel a financial pressure to work, whether or not they want to.

In 1920, a Royal Commission into wages determined what should be the basic wage for a family—that is, what a man should be paid to support a family consisting of himself, his wife and three children. The rate assumed that the family should be able to live in a five-roomed house with a reasonable yard, with bathroom and laundry facilities, situated in decent surroundings. The amount was adjusted up for those cities with higher real-estate prices. The wage also included the cost of clothing of "a good wearing quality as to fabric, and sound workmanship"; boots and shoes; groceries and other food (enough to provide calories for warmth and energy, a healthy weight and to meet the needs of growing children, as well as being palatable); fuel and light; household furnishings and utensils; doctor and dentist; domestic assistance; newspapers, stationery, and stamps; recreation, amusements and library; smoking; barber; fares; and school requisites.[26] In other words, a single wage was quite enough for a family to

---

25 'To Have and to Hold, p. 68.
26 See George Anderson, Fixation of Wages in Australia, Macmillan and Co., Melbourne, 1929.

live comfortably in the city of their choice—and this was the *minimum* wage for an unskilled worker. Professionals earned considerably more. If only conditions were the same now! A family living in a capital city on one wage now is most likely a family struggling to pay the rent and keep the children in school uniforms. Young couples complain that it now takes two wages to live in the suburb where their parents survived comfortably on one.

The business world, then, has acquired two workers for one family wage, where it used to get only one worker for that amount. Capitalism has profited from women entering the workforce, but women and their families have merely seen the value of their wages drop. It has always been hard work to look after a family. Now most women still have that responsibility—and no amount of electrical appliances make the housework disappear—but have to contribute financially as well. Debates over how equally the housework is divided between

Women who have dominated the nation's army of volunteers are rapidly taking on paid work in the welfare sector, threatening the supply of unpaid labour on which many services depend. In a "double-edged sword" for the expanding welfare sector, married women, especially those with children, are taking jobs in the community services field because of its high proportion of part-time work…the downside is that labour force participation among women threatens to deplete the supply of volunteer labour.

(THE AUSTRALIAN, 26/11/99)

husband and wife cannot conceal the basic problem, which is that women who work have not seen their lives become easier and more pleasant as the result of their labours, but rather more complicated and stressful.

Nonetheless, in popular reporting the increase in employment for women is frequently regarded as a triumph. According to the public face of women's issues, it is simply a matter of justice and something to be celebrated that so many women are now in the paid workforce—and a trend that should continue. Problems of stress and tiredness will, after all, be overcome as soon as men take on more of their share of the housework. However, when we look at what women actually want, we find quite a different trend. We do not see the majority of women wanting a full-time career and only half the care of the children.

According to the Australian Institute of Family Studies, of women working full-time, 43% wished for fewer hours. Of women who work, even those whose children are at school, a great many wish to work less—from full-time to part-time or less. Of women who do not work, regardless of the age of their children, only 5% wish for full-time employment.

The majority of women who work, want to work—but not full time or even close to full-time. The group of working mothers most content with their hours were working part-time.[27] Moreover, over 90% of families indicate that they have no additional need for child care.[28] This suggests that very few women want to work more than they do. It appears that it is not lack of childcare that keeps women out of the full-time workforce; they just don't want to go.

Even those without children are starting to voice the previously unheard of notion: that maybe husband and family is not such a bad alternative to the career path. American *Cosmo* magazine quotes a survey that 68% of 3,000 married and single young women said "they'd ditch work if they could afford to". In other words, "Women who used to abhor the Mommy Track now pray for it".[29]

---

27 Helen Glezer and Ilene Wolcott, 'Work and family values, preferences and practice', Australian Institute of Family Studies, 1997.

28 'Child Care, Australia, 1996', ABS no. 4402.0

29 Quoted in *The Sydney Morning Herald*, 20/6/2000.

Yet the social pressure to work continues. The public voice of commentators on the topic asserts that women want to work and should work, and parliament is lobbied to create incentives for mothers to work. Anything less is derided as discrimination against women. Writer Anne Summers states:

It is a regrettable measure of how equality of the sexes is still not accepted as a goal in modern-day Australia—and despite some conspicuous successes by some women, it is certainly not yet a reality. Why else would the Prime Minister feel entitled to say, as he did last week when welcoming reduced unemployment figures, that now women could return home from the work-force? He did not make a similar suggestion about men.[30]

Maybe this was because the Prime Minister thought that, unlike men, women might wish to return home from the workforce. He would have been right.

Many women today have an economic independence that they would not have dreamed of a century ago. They have the possibility of professional careers just as men have, and can expect to earn a great deal of money. If what women wanted was economic independence, to escape from the dependence that women have traditionally had on men, to a large extent they have now found it.

However, the price they have paid has been their freedom. For all the rhetoric of choice, social, legal and financial pressures now limit women's choice to the extent that they cannot choose to keep a household and care for their children. If women genuinely wished to be away from children and house and pursuing careers, this could be a good thing. However that is not what

---

30 *The Sydney Morning Herald*, 23/12/99.

women want. Against their wishes, they have been forced into a role in which they must take on more paid employment than they want, simply in order for the family to survive.

A WOMAN'S LIFE

We began this chapter with the story of a woman's suffering. Over a century later, we see a different picture of suffering. In the collapse of marriage and in work, conditions are such that many women are unhappy, lacking support, even abused and traumatized. In the public media, we tend to hear the anecdotes of the unusual women who manage to juggle career and family, and cope happily with the strain; we do not hear the stories of the majority who do not. Women are bearing the brunt of social forces which leave them confused and frustrated. A woman's life is full of unpleasant choices and hard realities.

There is a reason for the plight of women in today's society. Apart from the general economic and social changes which have affected all people, and many adversely, since the beginning of the twentieth century, women have had an additional burden. Behind these disparate problems that women face, there can be found a driving force. It is called, most inaptly, feminism.

Chapter 2

WHAT IS FEMINISM?

The statement at the end of the last chapter sounds rather extreme. Surely feminism cannot be so universally condemned. After all, it has always been a movement that aimed to *help* women, and still does. To label feminism as the force that has *hurt* women sounds at best ridiculous and at worst reactionary, not to mention rednecked.

Yet that is what I aim to demonstrate in this chapter—that modern feminism has at its core the two very changes in society that have led to massive suffering for women. The revolution for women's liberation that exploded across the Western world in the 1960s and 70s had two primary conscious goals—the necessity for women to have careers on the same terms as men, and the breakdown of traditional marriage. The key texts in the feminist revolution had various kinds of rhetoric and argument, but when it came to the practical directions that were recommended, work and marriage were primary targets.

Even so, we need to recognize that feminism is now far more than just a political movement for the rights of women. It is a disparate and diverse phenomenon. Some scholars explore different ways of writing history as well as searching out new histories to write. Others examine literary theory and the way women are seen in literature, as well as deconstructing the way literature and language is created at all. For some the very concept of 'woman' is too restrictive and needs to be de-politicized.

Some of these issues will be addressed later, but the feminism that will be examined in this chapter is the basic drive for equal rights for women that characterized especially the later half of the twentieth century. It is the feminism with which most of us are familiar, through newspaper articles, television, or press releases from feminist organizations. It is the feminism that says, basically, women ought to have the opportunity for economic independence and whatever career tracks men have; and they ought to have freedom from male oppression in relationships.

This wave of feminism took off with particular potency in the 1960s. Inspired by a number of polemical texts and driven by the anger fuelled by 'consciousness-raising' groups, women of the Western world began not just to question but to reject their traditional roles of wife, mother and homemaker. The development of the contraceptive pill gave a tremendous boost to the movement, making it physically possible to reject these roles in a way never available before. The twentieth century saw an unprecedented revolution in the way women thought about themselves and in what they were prepared to do about it.

Such an astonishing social upheaval needed considerable impetus. The philosophy of feminism made thousands of women completely change the nature of their lives, with political and social consequences that would change the lives of millions of women. This philosophy began in books. Although the emotions, that drove the movement came from hundreds of small discussion groups that brought women together to complain together and encourage one another to action, the ideas began in certain 'classic' texts of feminism that stated vehemently that women were unjustly treated. These texts changed the world.

One afternoon I was helping Mama to wash up; she was washing the plates, and I was drying; through the window I could see the wall of the barracks, and other kitchens in which women were scrubbing out saucepans or peeling vegetables. Every day lunch and dinner; every day washing-up; all those hours, those endlessly recurring hours, all leading nowhere: could I live like that? An image was formed in my mind, an image of such desolate clarity that I can still remember it today: a row of grey squares, diminishing according to the laws of perspective, but all flat, all identical, extending away to the horizon; they were the days and weeks and years.

(SIMONE DE BEAUVOIR,
MEMOIRS OF A DUTIFUL DAUGHTER)

THE SUFFERING OF A FRENCHWOMAN

In 1949 Simone de Beauvoir, a French novelist and lover of the existentialist philosopher Jean Paul Sartre, wrote a two-volume work called *The Second Sex*.[1] The book was not translated into English until 1953, and was not terribly well known until perhaps a decade later. It was to spark, however, a radical movement around the world.

The Second Sex went on to become a standard text of feminism, a modern classic, praised as an incisive, thoughtful, intelligent and far-seeing critique of the female state that cut through layers of hypocrisy and mythology. It has been praised as one of the most important works ever on the understanding of women: "the greatest single contribution on the subject",[2] and an "extraordinary achievement".[3] Multitudes of feminist writings quote the now famous first line of the second volume: "One is not born, but rather becomes, a woman".[4]

One wonders, however, how many have read any more than this one line of the book. For quite astoundingly given the reputation of the book, *The Second Sex* has little to recommend it as an analysis of women. It can only be surmised that it struck an emotional chord with sufficiently influential women to gain popularity. For in hindsight, *The Second Sex* is a bitter and turgid view of French life generalized to be a universal account of women, backed up by statements about anthropology and biology

---

1.   Simone de Beauvoir *The Second Sex,* Penguin Books NSW 1972 trans H. M. Parshley (first published in French 1949).

2.   Juliet Mitchell, *Women's Estate*, Penguin Books, Harmondsworth, 1971, p. 81.

3.   Sheila Rowbotham, *Woman's Consciousness, Man's World*, Penguin Books, Harmondworth, 1972, p. 10. Both Juliet Mitchell and Sheila Rowbotham were significant in starting the Women's Liberation movement in Britain: see Once a Feminist: Stories of a Generation (Interviews by Michelene Wandor), Virago, London, 1990.

4.   A recent instance is Naomi Wolf, *Promiscuities*, Chatto and Windus, London, 1997, p. 143.

which, even if they were scientifically acceptable at the time, have long since been discarded.

The first volume of *The Second Sex* is a study of what biology, psychoanalysis, historical materialism, prehistory and history reveal about the nature and state of women. As a project, this seems to be a worthy way to approach the subject. The contents page is impressive as a comprehensive way to study woman, with sections on what science, history and mythology have to tell us about the nature of woman. The actual data and argument provided, however, are far from convincing. It is not that everything de Beauvoir states is false; but whatever accurate information she gives is so mixed with unsupported speculation, and coloured by her own moral bias, that the result is anything but a scholarly study of women.

A feminist is someone who believes in women's rights.
(FROM SOPHIE GRILLET, *FEMINISM FOR TEENAGERS*)

For instance, de Beauvoir's account of how male-female relationships developed in prehistory is an interesting kind of imaginative psychology. The story she tells of how men and women related in nomadic and prehistoric farming culture is charming, but it has no shred of historical evidence to back it up. De Beauvoir, in fact, acknowledges this at the start of the section:

> *The accounts of the primitive forms of human society provided by ethnographers are extremely contradictory, the more so as they are better informed and less systematized. It is peculiarly difficult to form an idea of a woman's situation in the pre-agricultural period.*[5]

---

5. *The Second Sex*, p. 93.

Nonetheless, it seems that de Beauvoir is able to assert with confidence:

> *The primitive hordes had no permanence in property or territory... children were for them a burden, not a prized possession... the woman who gave birth, therefore, did not know the pride of creation; she felt herself the plaything of obscure forces, and the painful ordeal of childbirth seemed a useless or even troublesome accident.*[6]

Just how is she able to know how women *felt* about childbirth in this era? Or that (as she goes on to assert) the man's hunting was regarded as having supreme dignity, while a woman's giving birth was regarded as uncreative and dull? The answer, actually, is existentialist philosophy, not anthropological evidence: "An existentialist perspective has enabled us, then, to understand how the biological and economic condition of the primitive horde must have led to male supremacy."[7]

This bland assertion of what must have been the case in past times continues without benefit of footnotes, or indeed much evidence. De Beauvoir's comments on Old Testament and early Christian cultures, for example, show little familiarity with the relevant texts. Verses from Proverbs 31 are quoted to demonstrate how the Israelite woman was "kept in the confinement of domestic duties", despite the fact that the very same chapter also praises the woman who "considers a field and buys it; with the fruit of her hands she plants a vineyard... she perceives that her merchandize is profitable... strength and dignity are her clothing".[8] The account of late ancient and medieval culture informs us more of de Beauvoir's own moral preferences than of history. Protection of

---

6. *Ibid.*, p. 94.
7. *Ibid.*, p. 97.
8. Proverbs 31:16, 18, 25.

women, she insists, is actually a cover for enslavement; love can only be found in adultery as long as the institution of marriage lasts; and prostitution arose as the result of monogamy.

On the mythology of woman, de Beauvoir is just as imaginative. With examples from five authors, she confirms that men think of women in various inferior categories, diminishing her even when he supposedly venerates her. De Beauvoir's view is that man needs woman but is eternally disgusted by her.

> *Thus what man cherishes and detests first of all in woman— loved one or mother—is the fixed image of his animal destiny; it is the life that is necessary to his existence but that condemns him to the finite and to death...He wishes to venerate his mother and love his mistress; at the same time he rebels against them in disgust and fear.*[9]

There is no room in de Beauvoir's account for different men having different attitudes, or even for some men quite liking women; this underlying hatred, she considers, is fundamental.

At times the analysis reaches somewhat absurd extremes:

> *She is All, that is, on the plane of the inessential; she is all the Other. And, as the other, she is other than herself, other than what is expected of her. Being all, she is never quite this which she should be; she is everlasting deception, the very deception of that existence which is never successfully attained nor fully reconciled with the totality of existents.*[10]

The second volume of *The Second Sex* is devoted to different stages in a woman's life—childhood, girlhood, marriage, motherhood, old age. According to de Beauvoir, they are all uniformly awful. If indeed the anecdotes she gives are true, it seems she did know a

---

9. *The Second Sex*, pp. 197-8.
10. *Ibid.*, p. 229.

lot of terribly unhappy women. What strikes one most on reading this volume, however—if one has already read de Beauvoir's auto-biographical works—is how her 'universal' account of a woman's life strikingly resembles her own.[11] The childhood and relationship with her mother that she describes is, indeed, quite tortured. But how many women have experienced this apart from de Beauvoir herself? Maybe it is an accurate picture of growing up in early twentieth-century France—but we have no assurance we can even generalize that far. As far as the text goes, there is no evidence to say either way how valid this description of a woman's life is.

> *People call me a feminist whenever I express sentiments that differentiate me from a doormat.*
>
> (FROM SOPHIE GRILLET, *FEMINISM FOR TEENAGERS*)

De Beauvoir's account of a woman's life is so bleak it almost fails to sound real. On menstruation: "All the evidence agrees in showing that whether the child has been forewarned or not, the event always seems to her repugnant and humiliating".[12] On female friendship: "Young girls quickly tire of one another; they do not band together in their prison for mutual benefit; and this is one of the reasons why the company of boys is necessary to them." Young girls, she says, engage in eating disgusting things and self-mutilation. "These sado-masochistic performances are at once an anticipation of the sexual experience and a protest against it."[13]

De Beauvoir's views on marriage are equally despondent. "While being supposed to lend ethical standing to woman's erotic

---

11. See the first volume of her autobiography: Simone de Beauvoir, *Memoirs of a Dutiful Daughter*, Penguin Books, Harmondsworth, 1963; first published in French, 1958.

12. *Ibid.*, p. 335.

13. *Ibid.*, p. 377.

life, marriage is actually intended to suppress it."[14] "Marriage is obscene in principle in so far as it transforms into rights and duties those mutual relations which should be founded on a spontaneous urge."[15] "It is sheer hypocrisy to hold that a union based on convenience has much chance of inducing love; it is pure absurdity to maintain that two married persons, bound by ties of practical, social, and moral interest, will provide each other with sex satisfaction as long as they live."[16] Considering that she considers sexual relationships outside marriage as equally likely to fail, one can only wonder if her own relationship with Sartre had instilled this kind of bitterness.

De Beauvoir's description of the post-menopausal woman is entirely depressing. "With no future, she [the menopausal woman] still has about one half of her adult life to live."[17] Menopause is "mutilation", a "fated and irreversible process", the "fatal touch of death"; the woman will experience "anguish", "life already done", "delusions of persecution", "pathological jealousy".[18] The old woman at last sees the world clearly: "But if her experience enables her to unmask deceits and lies, it is not sufficient to show her the truth…In her thinking as in her acts, the highest form of liberty available to the woman parasite is stoical defiance of sceptical irony. At no time of life does she succeed in being at once effective and independent."[19]

> *A feminist is a woman who has actively sought and fought for rights of women.*
>
> (FROM SOPHIE GRILLET, *FEMINISM FOR TEENAGERS*)

---

14. *Ibid.*, p. 455.
15. *Ibid.*, p. 463.
16. *Ibid.*, p. 464.
17. *Ibid.*, p. 587.
18. *Ibid.*, pp. 587-90.
19. *Ibid.*, p. 608.

What, then, does de Beauvoir recommend to solve this terrible tragedy that is womanhood? As the reader might guess, de Beauvoir is against the idea of marriage: "Individuals are not to be blamed for the failure of marriage: it is the institution itself, perverted as it has been from the start".[20] The ideal relationship has none of the social or legal ties of marriage: "The couple should not be regarded as a unit, a closed cell; rather each individual should be integrated as such in society at large, where each (whether male or female) could flourish without aid; then attachments could be formed in pure generosity with another individual equally adapted to the group, attachments that would be founded upon the acknowledgment that both are free".[21]

For the real salvation for women, in de Beauvoir's view, is economic independence. More than anything else, women must independently support themselves and follow careers of their own. Enjoyable, fulfilling, even noble activity for a wife is not enough; it must be financially rewarded activity. Moreover, it must continue throughout the relationship, and it must be financially equal to the husband's input, not merely supplementary to it. "Many young households give the impression of being on a basis of perfect equality. But as long as the man retains economic responsibility for the couple, this is only an illusion."[22] That is, the goal of equality is in effect economic equality. This is what will stop women from being the 'second' sex; this is what will rescue women from their slavery. Additional measures such as freely available abortion, contraception, paid leave for pregnancy, and the State assuming charge of the children[23] would all aid this end. The ideal society would be that in which women would be "reared and trained exactly like men";

---

20. *Ibid.*, p. 497.
21. *Ibid.*, p. 497.
22. *Ibid.*, p. 498.
23. This would mean that children are not "abandoned" to their parents; *ibid.*, p. 734.

"erotic liberty was to be recognized by custom" and "woman was to be *obliged* to provide herself with other ways of earning a living" [apart from marriage; de Beauvoir's italics].[24]

Life is not perfect—there will always be tedium in everyday tasks, frustration in relationships and disappointment of dreams. Some elements of what de Beauvoir described ring true for women who still have to fold nappies and struggle with an imperfect husband. Most people struggle with problems of identity and fulfiment in life at some stage.

Simone de Beauvoir took her dissatisfaction in life—described painstakingly well in her autobiography—and turned it into a universal story. She was certainly entitled to publish her own lament; but it is not true of all women, and never was. Yet her diagnosis, to which she offered unworkable solutions, became one of the foundations of a social revolution. Her bitterness led other women into bitterness, and her advice on the dissolution of marriage and the need for women to be economically independent was to bear much fruit.

AMERICAN MYSTIQUE

As America moved into the twentieth century, it began to set models of womanhood and domesticity which would echo through the Western world. These models, however much they corresponded to real women's lives, were firmly based on consumerism and suburban life. The young wife could now contemplate a house full of domestic appliances which removed drudgery. Motherhood began

---

24. *Ibid.*, p. 733.

to become a profession with all manner of experts giving advice. Those women who were working were doing so in the expectation of finding a marriage partner. The ideal woman worker was the secretary; glamorous, making the boss's life run smoothly, with the reward of marriage for her faithful work.

It was a story with its roots before the Second World War. The basis of employment was the family wage—that one man would earn enough to support his family. This was a protection to working class women, who otherwise might be forced to work to enable the family to survive, or forced to raise children in poverty. On this basis, a married woman was not expected to work; her husband was already earning enough for her, so she did not have to. With the Second World War, however, men were not available for work. Women had to 'man' the factories.

> *Feminism is a critique of misogyny, the assumption of male superiority and centrality.*
> (CHRIS BEASLEY,
> *WHAT IS FEMINISM, ANYWAY?*)

At the end of the Second World War, women and men were sent home—men from the armies and women from the factories— and a new time of prosperity and hopefulness began. A new and energetic economy gave a level of material comfort previously unheard of, and the standard of living took a huge jump. This was the new reason for work; to be able to afford material luxuries. It is the story of the rise of suburbia and the middle classes. 'Normal' living suddenly rose to a new standard, including a private house, refrigerator and stove, and a private car. Women were exhorted to stay in the home for the sake of their returning servicemen. For the most part, they went. A widespread feeling of contentment and fulfilment was expressed in popular literature. It was as if the ideal society had been reached in middle-class America.

In 1963, a clinical psychologist and journalist called Betty Friedan published a book about American women.[25] The ideal society, she said, was hiding an insidious problem. It was "the problem that has no name"; a general malaise of dissatisfaction with life and domesticity amongst women who were supposed to have everything a woman wants. "Each suburban wife struggled with it alone", wrote Friedan. "As she made the beds, shopped for groceries, matched slipcover material, ate peanut butter sandwiches with her children, chauffeured Cub Scouts and Brownies, lay beside her husband at night, she was afraid to ask even of herself the silent question: 'Is this all?'"[26]

American women, in the glow of post-war consumerism, had taken on a highly segregated lifestyle, in which home and children were strictly separated from men and work. The average marriage age had dropped and the birthrate had soared. Mind you, despite this description of bland similarity, a third of American women were working; but Friedan's complaint was that very few were pursuing careers. They worked to support their husbands or sons (or themselves) through university. Otherwise, they were housewives, the envy of the world, with their beautiful homes and children, their appliances and supermarkets, and had found true feminine fulfilment.

This, Betty Friedan wrote, had been the dominant, if not exclusive, public image of women for the fifteen years after the Second World War. It was not just that women were mostly housewives; their position as such was gloried in and celebrated in popular literature. Nonetheless, Friedan claimed (with no footnotes), that at the same time psychiatrists and doctors had noticed more and more women coming to them with vague problems.

---

25. Betty Friedan, *The Feminine Mystique*, Penguin Books, London, 1965 (First published W. W. Norton 1963).
26. *Ibid.*, p. 13.

Betty Friedan, she said, began to investigate; and she found women all over America, in cities and country towns, expressing the same general discontent. It was a sense of incompleteness, of emptiness, of tiredness and anger for no reason. It was an utter incomprehension of why life was so bad when they had everything that was supposed to make it good.

The problem, Betty Friedan claimed, was that women were just bored with having such artificially constrained lives. They loved their children, but apart from children's activities they just had nothing to do. Their high level of affluence, and the availability of housework appliances and supermarkets, meant that there was no struggle to exist. Freed from such basic constraints, they had a great deal of energy to apply to the rest of life—but the rest of life was mostly artificially developed forms of survival tasks (cooking, sewing, home crafts). While these could be interesting, they did not take up the energy of these healthy, well-fed, affluent women. So they poured themselves into their children, running children's clubs, PTAs, Brownies and Scouts; producing, Betty Friedan also claimed, children with no capability to entertain themselves and no sense of responsibility. The new affluence of the middle class, it seemed, was difficult to adjust to. Friedan, however, saw this not as a factor of economic change, but of the social views concerning women.

> *"My mother, Miriam, was beautiful...She swam, played bridge, mahjong, tennis, golf...Our house was beautifully decorated...my mother's dresses and suits were tailored by her dressmaker to fit with elegant precision...But she never had anything that she thought was important to do. One year she would run the Sunday School, another year the women's division of the Community Chest."*
>
> (BETTY FRIEDAN WRITING OF HER MOTHER, *LIFE SO FAR*)

The Feminine Mystique, Betty Friedan's book, was to have a tremendous impact on a new wave of feminists. It was a well-written and ostensibly careful study, although relying mostly on anecdotal evidence. Essentially, Friedan's proposed solution for the plight of American women was to get them out of the home and back to work. They were not to neglect their families, she said, but were to take up meaningful work that would serve the community in some way. Only by doing such recognized, useful work could women find the fulfilment they did not have in their homes. In her final chapter 'A New Life Plan for Women', Friedan listed example after example of women who had, in their own way, found fulfilment through work. Many took up part-time or full-time jobs. One turned the bedroom that was going to be for a fifth child into a studio, and began painting. Several went back to college, often part-time.

Betty Friedan encouraged women to gather up their courage and deny their 'just-a-housewife' status:

> *This does not mean, of course, that she must divorce her husband, abandon her children, give up her home. She does not have to choose between marriage and career; that was the mistaken choice of the feminine mystique. In actual fact, it is not as difficult as the feminine mystique implies, to combine marriage and motherhood and even the kind of lifelong personal purpose that once was called 'career'. It merely takes a new life plan—in terms of one's whole life as a woman.*[27]

The other important thing was that the job had to be "a job that she can take seriously as part of a life plan, work in which she can grow as part of society". In other words, volunteer work or community work was not enough. It had to be something challenging

---

27. *Ibid.*, p. 297.

for a woman of intelligence, and it had to be paid. "Being paid is, of course, more than a reward—it implies a definite commitment". Women had to make a serious professional commitment to their career in a lifelong plan. The actual form of the commitment might change according to circumstances: "a full-time paid job in one community, part-time in another, exercise of the professional skill in serious volunteer work or a period of study during pregnancy or early motherhood when a full-time job is not feasible".[28]

What a pity Betty Friedan did not foresee the results. This idyllic notion of popping in and out of full-time work was not going to happen in a competitive economic system. Capitalism is far more powerful than Friedan realized, it seems. Instead of a true choice to work or not, women are forced to face the impossibility of full-time career and motherhood, but are often without the economic freedom of giving up work to look after children. The professional workforce is generally very unfriendly to mothers, often demanding long hours and long weeks. Friedan did nothing to challenge this. Friedan's work also did not predict what was to become all too real a problem, as we have seen in chapter 1— that mothers would be pressured to work even when they do not

> *"Many women I know, who once disdained their mothers' lifestyles, no longer see those lives as boring and indulgent. Now, they look back with a tad of longing. Wouldn't it be pleasant to while away time playing bridge and tennis and lunching with girlfriends and eating shrimp cocktails and napping and taking the kids up to the beach house all summer and chilling the cocktail shaker when hubby's on his way home?"*
>
> (*THE NEW YORK TIMES*, 2000)

---

28. *Ibid.*, pp. 300-302.

want to. As feminist commentator Anne Summers has recently observed, "...domestic violence against women is at record levels and women are still concentrated in part-time, non-permanent, lower-paid jobs and increasing numbers of professional women fear to have babies because, despite legal protections, it might jeopardize their hard-won jobs. Women, it seems, just can't win."[29]

Not only that, but the satisfying life that 'career' was supposed to bring has not eventuated for many women who believed the promises. Work can be a high-pressure grind just as much as any fulfilling freedom, and many women wonder if the 'victory' of a high-powered career was worth it. They may have proved they were capable of a successful work life, but it can result in a very lonely life. One woman writes of the real anguish some of her friends face:

> Housework and the raising of children, denigrated by the movement and by so many elite women, is looked upon very differently by my unmarried friends, even those who call themselves feminists...The tragic part is the egocentrism of their current existence, the days and years devoted to self-maintenance, with minimal effects on the lives of others. Women now get to fulfil themselves...but they do so in the most resolute solitude.[30]

What's more, too many women have absorbed the debilitating message that a lifelong professional career is the only way to be fulfilled and worthwhile, making any desire for, or commitment to, full-time motherhood a weak or even foolish option. Economic forces are not the only ones that push women into unwanted work.

---

29. SMH 23/12/99.
30. Elizabeth Powers, 'A farewell to feminism', *Commentary Magazine*, January 1997.

It is precisely the kind of rhetoric that Friedan used which has made being a mother into a non-activity. Friedan taught the capitalist myth that the only worthwhile work is paid work—that 'work' done at home, for free, is not really work at all. Women themselves have internalized that myth. A newspaper report on single mothers includes the astonishing statement from the mother of a pre-schooler that sole parents of school-aged children have no excuse to "sit at home". "You are not a full-time mother when your kid starts school", she says. "And I think married women with school-aged children who stay home are lazy, too. With before-and-after school care available, there's no excuse."[31] Even 'expert' opinion is now that mothers *ought*, as a social obligation, to work.

> *The Best Man for the Job*
> *May Be a Woman.*
> (NOW BUMPER STICKERS)

> *The traditional liberal view was that a mother performed a social task by raising her child, and she should be supported to do that. But since the '60s, most mothers have taken jobs alongside raising their children, so we no longer think it fair that welfare mothers not have to work too.*[32]

Not only are mothers who care for their children at home poorer, they are now lazy and without excuse as well. With Betty Friedan's book, the march towards the stressed and constrained lifestyle for women was on the way.

---

31. SMH 16/3/00.
32. Lawrence Mead, US specialist on welfare reform, SMH 25/07/2000.

FROM BETTY FRIEDAN TO NOW

Betty Friedan's book was hardly the sound, frank discussion it presented itself as. Friedan appeared in her book as the concerned, helpful friend who had been through the struggle of being an unfulfilled housewife and wanted to share with others her solution to the problem. The reality was rather different. She described herself as a suburban housewife who had lived out the feminine mystique herself, suffered from the same imprisonment and boredom. She failed to mention her highly successful academic career and her subsequent career as a professional journalist, which she continued along with political activities while she married and moved to the suburbs. Far from falling prey to the feminine mystique, entrapped by boredom and powerlessness, Friedan was an extremely active and powerful woman. In her own life she demonstrated that the feminine mystique—if it existed at all—was hardly overwhelming.

Personal experience was not the only basis Betty Friedan gave for her views. She offered academic support for her ideas; citing intellectuals such as anthropologist Margaret Mead, psychologist Sigmund Freud and sex researcher Alfred Kinsey. That list of 'experts', however, now reads rather sadly. Mead's work in Samoa has now been considerably undermined by the finding that some of her informants deliberately lied to her. Freud's psychology has been almost totally superseded. Kinsey's data has been shown to be seriously flawed and his sampling unrepresentative.

However, Friedan's reading audience had no such qualms (and her book is still cited as a feminist classic). Women, recognising their imprisonment, went out to make things better for themselves—by taking up paid careers. Following Friedan's advice meant not going out to make things better for other people, or trying to overcome isolation by finding other isolated women and doing what they could to help them and the community they lived in; Friedan's message was that the only real work was paid work, and the message reached American women and others around the world. The new truth for women was that being at home was to be trapped, powerless, dull and meaningless; whereas professional work was good, interesting, and necessary in order to be a real human being. Even if housewives were not feeling discontent beforehand, once this message began to permeate society they began to be.

It was also, of course, a very white and middle-class analysis. Black women living in inner-city communities had not been suffering from the problem without a name. There was a growing population of ethnic urban poor struggling for work, and women often were forced to work in poorly-paid jobs in order for their families to survive. These women were not bored with life; their work was a matter of survival, not fulfilment. The movement that was about to shake middle-class America would not affect them, except to proclaim goals for women which they could not possibly hope to achieve. Yet amongst middle-class urbanites, Betty Friedan was hugely influential. The shape of modern feminism was here.

As the 1960s began, all sorts of accepted orthodoxies were under challenge in Western ideology. Colonial nations were asserting independence, and insisting they were aligned neither with Russia nor the United States. Beatniks protested the nuclear age and criticized materialism. The 'sexual revolution' attacked traditional models of relationships, and women found opportunity for sexual experimentation. Female students joined with their male colleagues to protest violence. At the same time, the workplace began to change for women. President Kennedy appointed a Presidential Commission on the Status of Women. Their report was issued in 1963 and resulted in a presidential order requiring the civil service to hire solely on the basis of ability, without regard to sex. Also in the same year—before major feminist pressure—the Equal Pay Act made it illegal to have different rates of pay for women and men for the same work.

Coming in conjunction with such reforms, *The Feminine Mystique* had a stunning impact. Betty Friedan was overwhelmed with the volume of mail she received from women who had read her book. A new Equal Employment Opportunity Commission (created after the legal prohibition against discrimination in employment was changed to include sex as well as race, creed and nationality) was deluged with cases. Betty Friedan and other prominent feminists feared that the Commission would be unable to police the discrimination it was uncovering, and so NOW, the National Organization for Women, was created in Betty Friedan's hotel room over lunch in 1966.

NOW began agitating for the enforcement of the new antidiscrimination laws. It was essentially a political lobby group, self-consciously a group for women, professional women in particular. The founding statement held that women should not be expected to devote the greater part of their lives to child-rearing; a large part of the concerns dealt with getting more women into the workplace. Betty Friedan writes in her autobiography that she was conscious of starting something radical and new that would change society: "we're going to start a woman's movement".[33]

Explain to Me Again Why I Need a Man.

(NOW BUMPER STICKERS)

Out of NOW grew the American women's liberation movement in general. A new generation of young women, radical and angry, asserted the need for personal support for women and a

---

33. Betty Friedan, *Life So Far*, Simon and Schuster, New York, 2000, P. 178

new philosophy of womanhood. They wanted community and sisterhood, not just equal pay (which in any case had been won without their activism). Their cry 'the personal is political' characterized this. The problem, they insisted, was not just economic or legal inequality. It was to do with the whole way women were perceived, their character and place in society, and what their lives were meant to be.

Many of these women had been active in various social movements throughout the sixties. Civil rights, protests against Vietnam, and demonstrations for peace had involved both men and women in highly organized social action. Women had wanted more than that, however. In 1967, Shulamith Firestone, who was to become a leading feminist writer and agitator, left a conference of the Student Non-Violence Coordinating Committee (which had done considerable work on behalf of civil rights) to organize a separate movement for women. There were already networks of activist women across the country; these women became the first members of the new 'consciousness-raising' groups set up throughout America. One woman reports the power of these discussion groups:

> It was tremendously exciting. We felt like we were breaking through our conditioning and learning new things each week. Maybe small groups have this same experience now, but I think there was probably more tension and emotion because of the newness of it all—no one else seemed to have heard of Women's Liberation—we were freaks. I used to be exhausted and exhilarated after meetings and used to lie awake thinking—couldn't stop.[34]

This was to be one of the most brilliant political strokes of the fem-

---

34. Letter from a member of one of the first consciousness-raising groups in London, formed by American women, June 1971. Quoted in *Once a Feminist: Stories of a Generation* (Interviews by Michelene Wandor), Virago, London, 1990, p. 18.

inist movement. In these discussion groups, women presented their grievances to a sympathetic audience and would be encouraged in their rebellion against whatever held them down. Anger was stoked, and then directed into activism. Feminists staged demonstrations, leafleted, published papers and made a lot of noise. New groups could be set up by anyone, and immediately appealed to many women. They ranged from working women to the wives of congressmen. In these groups, the personal lives of women *became* political as what they shared about their lives became a basis for protest. Women's Lib had begun.

AUSTRALIAN INFLUENCE

In 1970, a young Australian named Germaine Greer published a book that attacked many of the same issues that *The Feminist Mystique* had, but with a much higher level of anger. In *The Female Eunuch*, Greer promoted sexual activity as something far broader than marriage and motherhood. Greer criticized Friedan's tendency to "stress non-sexual aspects of a woman's destiny at the expense of her libido" and rather scathingly rejected NOW's "token reforms".[35] Such sentiments, written only seven years after *The Feminine Mystique*, show how quickly feminism was moving.

Germaine Greer's solutions to the female problem were far more radical than Betty Friedan's. She was not advocating traditional family plus part-time college: "If women are to effect a significant amelioration in their condition it seems obvious that

---

35. Friedan, in turn, regards *The Female Eunuch* as "a combination of good stuff and a sort of naughty child exhibitionism"; and if Greer could not understand Friedan's failure to emphasise sexuality as the major issue of women's liberation, Friedan says "Germain had written all about sexual politics in *The Female Eunuch*, but she had no interest in women's major concern—employment". Betty Friedan, *Life so Far, op. cit.*, p. 284. This illustrates well the two major thrusts of feminist activism.

they must refuse to marry". Did a woman want children? "If a woman marries because she wants to have children, she might reflect that the average family has not proved to be a very good breeding ground for children, and seeing as the world is in no urgent need of her increase she might do better, for contraception is very possible, to wait until some suitable kind of household presents itself". This "suitable" household might be single motherhood, or friendly cohabitation with another. Such situations undoubtedly would bring "outrage and persecution", but "marrying to avoid these inconveniences is a meaningless evasion". For the married woman without children, she must insist upon her rights and give up her fear of abandonment. "It is largely a question of nerve", Greer wrote; and women's societies should be able to help in stirring up the right amount of "nerve". For mothers, of course, the situation was more difficult: "yet women with children do break free, with or without their offspring". Again women's organizations would help; and in any case "brutally clear rethinking" must take place about a woman's responsibilities to her children.[36]

In other words, Germaine Greer advocated that women choose *any* kind of living situation other than marriage. Greer told women that they did not have a responsibility to their children, and certainly not to a husband. A women's prime and overriding responsibility was to herself. Women were told to do whatever it was they felt like, throw off any arrangement that felt constricting. Germaine Greer challenged women to fight the status-quo in which, she considered, women were almost inevitably denigrated and suppressed by men. It was a woman's duty; the married woman *must*, Greer wrote, "fight the guilt of failure in an impossible set-up, and examine the set-up". Her sisters would

---

36. Germaine Greer, *The Female Eunuch*, Paladin, London, 1971, pp. 319-322.

support her in her analysis of her problems; at the same time she must resist discussing her situation with her husband, who would only "ridicule and baffle" her. Most of all, she must not allow herself "to be blackmailed by his innocence of his part in her plight and his magnanimity in offering to meet her half-way in any 'reasonable' suggestions".[37]

So not even reasonable discussion was allowed. Ideology was overriding reality with a vengeance. It didn't matter, in Greer's advice, if a woman's husband was generous, innocent of wrong, willing to compromise and wanting to be reasonable. No matter *how* good he was, he had to be left. He was not to be told about it—Greer did not want any chance of women being "ridiculed and baffled" (a rather condescending view of women). The poor husband, not aware of having done anything wrong, would just have to watch his wife become more and more angry and then leave, refusing to tell him what was wrong. There didn't have to be anything wrong. Marriage itself, Greer taught, was wrong.

THE PERSONAL BECOMES POLITICAL

Political and legal reforms followed fast in the 1970s. Some reforms were positive. Equal pay legislation was fought for.[38] Domestic violence and rape were identified as particular problems, and social and legal solutions were demanded. Discrimination was sought out and attacked in places of work and learning. Women's anger appeared in marches, demonstrations,

---

37. *Ibid.*, p. 322.
38. Actually equal pay had already been introduced in certain Western countries during World War II in order to protect men's jobs in certain trades. It gradually spread through society as economic policy changed from the needs-based pay structure of the early twentieth century—in itself not necessarily an unfair policy—to the individualistic policy of the late twentieth century.

magazine articles, strikes and arguments while individual feminists continued their sensational protests and publicity-raising stunts. It was an anger that could only spread; women were caught up in the anger as they reflected upon injustices in their own lives. The consciousness-raising groups in fact raised high emotions and changed women into activists.

It is perhaps because of the consciousness-raising groups more than anything else that there was such an incredible spread of feminist ideas and arguments throughout the seventies. While a great many people—probably the majority, male and female—of the Western world remained hostile or indifferent to feminist ideas, feminism's advance into Western ideology proceeded at an astonishing rate. Bastion after bastion fell; feminist ideas were introduced into university curricula, school policies, and family discussions. The question was not just about women's rights, nor just women's roles. It was a radical rethinking of the nature of woman in most general terms. It was a rethinking perhaps not possible amongst feminists of an earlier generation, not just because of social opposition and economic restrictions, but also because of the lack of reliable contraception, which did keep women in motherhood or abstinence. With the freedom of easy contraception, and the possibility of legal abortion after the famous *Roe vs Wade* case in 1973, women could potentially throw off everything that women had traditionally been. Such freedom, totally unknown in previous societies, made for radical proposals. The more discussion there was, the more old ideological barriers seemed to be obsolete, and the more possibilities for womanhood there seemed to be.

Rape crisis centres and battered women's centres were set up to take in victims. Women set up publishing houses, academic journals and collectives. The battle for women's ordination within mainline churches began with writers such as Mary Daly and Rosemary Radford Reuther, who rejected traditional theology and set up new, woman-based ways of doing theology. Central doctrines such as 'God the Father' were attacked and even dismissed altogether. Female linguists battled over issues of gender-neutral or gender-free language. Academics instituted new areas of study, reclaiming women's history and beginning feminist literary theory.

THE FRACTURING OF FEMINISM

As we look at the more academic feminist writing that has appeared since the 1970s, we begin to see ideas that seem almost from a different universe from Betty Friedan's polite reflections on housewives. Consider a quotation from the feminist movement twenty years after Friedan:

> ...*two important theses for further development by feminist thinkers... [are] compulsory heterosexuality is the central social structure perpetuating male domination... [and] a reconstruction of the concept* lesbian *in terms of a cross-cultural, transhistorical lesbian continuum which can capture women's ongoing resistance to patriarchal domination.*[39]

Equal-rights feminism enjoyed considerable success, but as time went on the considerable differences of opinion in the ranks began to be felt. With an agenda which was now so broad as to include everything about women, including the very definition of what a woman was, it is not surprising that widely differing views and priorities began to emerge. Abortion and lesbianism were particularly contentious issues. Many women began to use their raised consciousness to oppose issues such as these, which

---

39. Ann Fergusen, 'Patriarchy, sexual identity, and the sexual revolution', *Signs*, 1981, 7, pp. 158-172, p. 158.

other feminists held to be central. One feminist reflects:

> *Probably then (1974) I did have a sense of there being two strands in the women's movement, that the women's liberation ones were more likely to be about sexual orientation— whether the women's movement was sufficiently attentive to lesbians…Then there were the socialist feminist conferences which were much easier. They were obviously more to do with demands and trying to formulate a future for women that the maximum number of women could agree to.[40]*

As political feminists became more powerful, divisions began to emerge about precisely what laws would help women most. Should laws be gender neutral? Should there be special laws for women? Would this help women, or reinforce a stereotype that women need to be protected? Should there be maternity leave or parental leave? Should divorce laws favour women?

Another issue on which feminists split widely was pornography—some seeing it as a celebration of female sexuality, others condemning it as exploitation of women. As reproductive technology improved, whole new battlegrounds were formed. Was it a freedom or a potential exploitation that surrogate mothers were now possible? Opinions differed, because of course such technologies could be both. In an era where children became a commodity which could be bought, discarded, planned or postponed, and in which traditional models of family had been deliberately discarded, there were no guidelines. A great many feminists faced the quandary that they knew what they *didn't* want, but not what they *did*; and what they had did not seem to be working.

There is hardly a feminist movement today. While certain organizations such as NOW exist, feminism is much more a way

---

40. Janet Ree, in Once a Feminist: Stories of a Generation, *op. cit.*, pp. 101-102.

of thinking, or a way of approaching certain topics, than a movement. While lesbian academics discuss whether 'woman' exists, female politicians still talk about getting more women into parliament. There is no united battle front any more. Hundreds of lobby groups and individuals follow their own goals, and, as long as these goals somehow impinge upon women, they are able to attach the label 'feminist'. Within this label can be found totally contradictory ideas. Is it feminist to want equal relationships with men, separate realms from men, power over men or to do away with men? At the same time, policies instituted or argued for as 'feminist' lead to practical impossibilities: should the state pay welfare to single mothers, or pay for childcare while they work, and why is either condition regarded as 'independence'? Even specialists cannot agree what feminism is any more:

> *There is little disagreement among feminists that many kinds of feminist thought exist but feminists have offered widely different accounts of the ways in which they are divided and whether or not these divisions are important.*[41]

REALITY CHECK

Let us pause for a moment and compare the aims of feminism with its achievements. The more practical feminist programs have aimed at such things as helping single mothers and children out of poverty, ending violence against women, ending abuse of children, and so on. These are certainly admirable ends. However many of these goals do not sit well with feminist policies.

---

41. Chris Beasley, *What is feminism, anyway? Understanding Contemporary Feminist Thought*, Allen and Unwin, Sydney, 1999, p. 41. See also Jean Curthoys *Feminist Amnesia: The Wake of Women's Liberation*, Routledge, London and New York, 1997, for the confusion that now plagues feminism.

For example, by far the best way to reduce violence against children generally is to encourage marriage, as we have seen in the first chapter. There may be disastrous stories of abuse within marriage, but the statistics show that there are considerably more without marriage. The best way to end poverty for single mothers is to provide incentives for them to marry. There could be no in-principle objection to provide incentives for single mothers to change their way of life; after all, Western governments are now bringing pressure to bear on single mothers to work. So why not to do what would best help them and their children—find a husband who can support them?

Yet this is precisely what NOW is against. A recent press release proclaims:

> *Congress wants to reduce poverty by giving money to programs that support non-custodial fathers hoping that some of that money will trickle-down to needy kids…the Fathers Count Act would only fund programs that 'promote marriage'.*[42]

NOW, in this press release, criticizes congress for supporting the Fathers Count Act which only funds programmes that promote marriage, because this is telling women that "the way to get out of poverty is to find a husband". However, as uncomfortable as the reality may be, finding a husband *is* the best way out of poverty for women. Study after study has shown this to be true.[43] NOW also objects because the Fathers Count Act is "allowing father's rights groups to advance their agenda with money that should be used to help poor children". Having a father *does* help poor children. It could well be argued that if you care about children, you will want to penalize those who bear children in an irresponsible manner, and support those who are prepared to make personal

---

42. NOW press release, 30/10/99.
43. See, for instance, ABS no. 6224.0, already cited in chapter 1.

and financial sacrifices for their children. In that case, one can only wonder how much feminist groups such as NOW really care about children—or women.

What exactly were feminists trying to achieve through feminism? If it was a better life for women, they have not succeeded—and they continue to agitate for further reforms that ignore the data about what women need. This is merely one example of the gulf between the claims of feminism and the reality of women's lives.[44]

The agenda of equal rights feminism has been expressed in many ways since the 1960s. However the two major differences which its advocates wanted to see in society were women working in the paid world alongside men, and women not being confined to marriage with men. These two issues in particular were seen as crucial to women's subjugation by men—that men prevented them from earning the money they needed, and men imprisoned women in family life. These issues were meant to be central to women's experience of life. Getting women out of the family home and into the workforce was supposed to solve women's problems—make them happier, more satisfied, stronger, more fully human than before.

I loved The Female Eunuch. *I thought it was brilliant when I read it.*

(ERICA JONG, QUOTED IN SUSAN MITCHELL, *ICONS, SAINTS AND DIVAS*)

There certainly are many freedoms for women today—freedom to have sex without marriage, without the risk of children and without social stigma; freedom to live with someone before mar-

44. Germaine Greer has herself acknowledged many ways in which modern 'equality' for woman has not lived up to its aims; see for instance her comments on corporate working life in her recent book *The Whole Woman*, Alfred A. Knopf, New York, 1999, pp. 340-341.

riage; freedom to change partners, and to divorce easily; freedom to have children out of wedlock. Yet these are not freedoms that all women find beneficial. Single motherhood is a very difficult life for most women. Divorce hurts children, hurts their mothers and usually leaves them poorer, according to current research. Yet feminism is now so established as an ideology in our society, these awkward facts are rarely mentioned. A newspaper article laments that a woman is facing poverty because her marriage has broken down. The article suggests that work laws and things like maternity leave need to be changed. Yet the key issue—that divorce leaves women in poverty, despite reforms in divorce laws—is not even addressed.[45] It seems that feminism has blinded many social commentators to basic cause and effect. Feminism was supposed to work. It was supposed to make women's lives better. How could it possibly be the cause of women's suffering?

> *The other day my friend and I were just chatting and she said that if she had to be a housewife she wouldn't mind it and I really couldn't understand that, because I would never ever want to be a housewife, because it's like buying into the idea that men are dominant because you're working for them.*
>
> (JULIA PRESS, IN ON THE MOVE: FEMINISM FOR A NEW GENERATION)

Feminism, it now seems, was based on a myth—that women used to be particularly downtrodden and unhappy, but by

---

45. SMH 16/2/99. This is only one of many such examples of selective interpretation due to feminist prejudice that I have found in researching this book. For a detailed study of some of the mistakes of feminist writings, see Christina Hoff Sommers, *Who Stole Feminism? How Women have Betrayed Women*, Simon and Schuster, New York and others, 1994.

demanding economic and relational independence from men they could now be happy. Of course life has never been perfect. But the analysis that proclaimed that women's problems would be overcome by escaping marriage and domesticity in particular, was always misguided. It is an extremely powerful myth, and it has taken over universities, public media, primary schools, politics and home life. It always *sounded* good. Yet on any objective reading of the data, it has yielded dreadful consequences for society in general and women in particular. What was wrong with it?

⊶ *Chapter 3* ⊷

THE FEMINIST MIND

Photo: Simone de Beauvoir

Where did feminism go wrong? How did a movement with ostensibly admirable aims—to improve women's lives and work for justice—contribute to such dire social consequences? To begin to answer this, we must look at the philosophical basis of the feminist movement—the basic assumptions about what is good in life and how to achieve the good life for women. We need to understand what was the driving philosophical force behind the arguments of the feminist movement.

Most feminist activism, it must be said, has been philosophically poor.[1] Of more recent years, academic feminism has taken on philosophy but generally of a deconstructionist kind, which is much better at defining what is not than what is. The more prominent feminism, which lobbies to change laws and which reaches the general public, usually starts from a simple claim for freedom and justice to women, rather than from a substantial philosophical analysis of life. A typical statement might be:

> *To me, feminism is about finding equality between men and women in all areas of society, from work to family situations, without women being seen as the weaker sex.*[2]

Yet if we are to understand the essence of feminism, we need to know feminism's answer to two basic philosophical questions. The first is, what is the ultimate goal of life? For this determines

---

1. There is certainly plenty written under the heading "feminist philosophy". However this is not the philosophy of feminism in the sense used here. It is generally an attempt to establish an uniquely feminist position on, or critique of, existing philosophical problems (which often fails—see, for instance, Cassandra L. Pinnick, 'Feminist philosophy of science: high hopes', *Metascience*, 2000, *9*, pp. 257-266). What I claim here is that the social movement of feminism which has influenced the Western world since the 1960s is rarely presented with a coherent philosophy which would justify its own political and social claims for women.

2. Karen Loughrey, 'You go girl!—young women say there's no holding back', in Natasha Walter (ed.), *On the move: Feminism for a New Generation*, Virago Press, London, 1999, p. 5.

what should be the ultimate goal of every human being, including women. The second question is, what is a woman? In order to fight for women's right to achieve the ultimate goal of human beings, it is necessary to know for whom we are fighting and therefore how to fight for them.

Does this matter? Surely the actions are more important than obscure philosophy? It *does* matter, because feminism insists that it represents the right way to live life and to direct society. But how do we know that it is the right way? What *is* the ultimate good for people, and is feminism heading in that direction? It is easy to assume that catch phrases such as 'rights', 'freedom', and 'equality' are good goals, but without explaining what each of these terms mean, we cannot judge whether they are what we want for people.

In fact, a lot of the confusion in feminism—the different kinds of feminism, from lesbian separatists to working mothers—stems from the fact that the ultimate good of humanity is rarely spelt out in any consistent way. Feminism therefore usually degenerates into whatever women want, and since there are a lot of different women, that amounts to a lot of contradictory goals.

Given that the philosophical assumptions are rarely spelt out, it is a little difficult, then, to know where to look for a philosophical basis for feminism that we can evaluate. There is one place, however, where such a basis has been clearly explained, and since this is in a book which is widely acclaimed as a feminist classic and a motivator for many leading feminists, I will take it as a good example of feminist theorising. That is, Simone de Beauvoir's *The Second Sex*.

WHAT DO WE WANT FROM LIFE?

Simone de Beauvoir was a highly educated philosopher; she was as well qualified as Jean Paul Sartre, and like him taught philosophy for years before turning to an exclusively literary career. She did not develop any notable philosophy of her own, but followed Sartre's ideas, considering them groundbreaking and ultimately true. Her views on women, then, were based on this well-thought-out philosophy, and she took pains to explain and clarify her conclusions.

The question that needs to be answered, before we come to consider "what is the ultimate good for women", is "what is the ultimate good for humanity". According to Simone de Beauvoir, this is an undetermined, unrestricted freedom. "There is no justification for present existence other than its expansion into an indefinitely open future."[3] That is, the only thing that makes life worth living is the capacity for it to be anything in the future. As long as there is restriction upon a person—financial, social, family or whatever—that person is not living a life true to themselves. To improve a life is to remove restrictions and enable openness and freedom. This is what de Beauvoir refers to as *transcendence*—getting beyond the mundane inanities of day-to-day life, having the freedom to dream and live out dreams, be more than just a survivor and become someone who truly lives.

These writers and their books have taught us all to ask as women, 'How far can I go? How much can I achieve?' and to stretch the boundaries of possibility, to leap the barrier, to push out the envelope, to crack through the glass ceiling, to go where other women have feared to tread. To be brave enough to be yourself or the self you secretly want to become. As Robin Morgan's poem said, 'There is nothing you cannot be'.

(SUSAN MITCHELL, *ICONS, SAINTS AND DIVAS*)

---

3. Simone de Beauvoir, *The Second Sex, op. cit.*, pp. 28-29.

64

This, she claims, is what men have and what women are precluded from having. Women are trapped in *immanence*, trapped in the moment, in unimportant things. "Immanence... is an absolute evil." This is what must be escaped.

This immanence for women began, according to de Beauvoir, in prehistoric times. (Although there is no reason to suppose this is historically accurate, it does serve to illustrate the philosophy we are discussing.) The woman in a nomadic tribe would be weakened by constant pregnancy; and since for nomads there is no posterity gained by passing on property, the children would not be valued. The woman, then, knew the painful ordeal of childbirth with no pride of creation. The domestic labours that were reconcilable with the cares of maternity became hers, and these imprisoned her in repetition and immanence. Man, however, supported the group by means of acts that transcended his animal nature: the inventor, the explorer, the creator. He had festivals to celebrate his triumphs. He broke through frontiers and laid down a new future. Also, his activity was dangerous. In risking his life for the sake of the tribe, he demonstrated his superiority above the animals.

Forever since, the man transcends life while the woman only repeats life. "Her misfortune is to have been biologically destined for the repetition of Life, when even in her own view Life does not carry within itself its reasons for being, reasons that are more important than the life itself."[4] The essential problem is that women are kept from doing the kind of worthwhile things that achieve transcendence.

> One of the basic problems of woman, as we have seen, is the reconciliation of her reproductive role and her part in productive labour. The fundamental fact that from the beginning of his-

---

4. *Ibid.*, p. 96.

tory doomed woman to domestic work and prevented her tak-
ing part in the shaping of the world was her enslavement to the
generative function.[5]

Men have always kept power to themselves, de Beauvoir goes on. This suited the economic interests of the males and also their ontological and moral pretensions to superiority. The irony is, however, that woman cannot fill his needs. It is only the existence of other men that tears each man out of his immanence and enables him to fulfil the truth of his being. Friendship and generosity alone permit the recognition of free beings, and so one is able to find his true nature. In the slave called 'woman' he cannot find friendship and so cannot find himself.

But this true nature is unceasing struggle. The transformation through which he attains true wisdom is never done. And man does not like difficulty; he aspires in contradictory fashion both to life and to repose. So woman for him becomes his dream of repose; one without the hard requirement of a reciprocal relation, but still with consciousness. No man wants to be a woman but every man wants women to exist; by keeping her in immanence, he can enjoy his transcendence. Also de Beauvoir sees man's desire for transcendence as being a revolt against nature, to become "like a pure Idea, like the One, the All, the absolute Spirit", something which is "imprisoned by woman in the mud of the earth".[6] Man would like to deny his animal ties, but woman keeps on reminding him of them.

Childbirth, says de Beauvoir, has always been greeted with a kind of revulsion. The little boy tries to tear himself away from his mother, dislikes her caresses, because, "To have been conceived and then born an infant is the curse that hangs over his

---

5. *Ibid.*, p. 148.
6. *Ibid.*, p. 177.

destiny, the impurity that contaminates his being. And, too, it is the announcement of his death."[7] In turn, mothers become the oppressors who, ashamed of their state, seek to make converts in order to justify themselves. At the same time, the little girl learns that in order to be happy she must be loved, and in order to be loved she must wait for love to turn up. She feels transcendent but it is revealed to her that she is inferior. The boy looks at an open future in which he can be anything, but the girl sees her future already written: mother, grandmother.[8]

By the time the woman becomes a wife and mother, she is firmly stuck in her immanence. "Because she *does* nothing, she eagerly seeks self-realization in what she *has*."[9] So for de Beauvoir, the ultimate reason why being a housewife is bad is because it profoundly and ultimately denies what is the goal of all humankind. "What makes the lot of the wife-servant ungrateful is the division of labour which dooms her completely to the general and the inessential."

So what should women do? Try anything to escape what keeps them in immanence—motherhood, housework, dependence on men. This is the reason for feminist activity; this is the philosophy which justifies the struggle for personal and economic independence.

What do we make of this philosophy? It is certainly rigorous in a way that most popular feminism is not; it has given a basis and grounding for activism. However there are certain ironies, not to mention plain impossibilities, in taking this on as a life philosophy.

Take, for instance, the point that women are constantly kept

---

7. *Ibid.*, p. 179.
8. *Ibid.*, p.325. Aspects of this are expanded upon in chapter 2 of Book 2, 'The Young Girl'.
9. *Ibid.*, p. 469.

in the mundane and ordinary world by their reproductive links to reality. This is certainly true. Reproduction *is* a reminder of mortality. Woman's own life traditionally is a constant reminder to her of death. Not only does childbirth risk death, but the birth itself is a reminder that life is not eternal, but begins and ends. Now, however, with technology she wipes out her own reminder. So now woman can seek transcendence too. Is this not, however, somewhat ironic? For death is still there; technology can hide the reminders, but cannot take reality away. If the achievement of transcendence, the worthwhile life, requires wiping out all traces of reality, it is not much of a transcendence. It is just as illusory for her as it always was for man. What's more, now woman can show contempt for those women who choose not to deny these reminders.

The question is whether you choose to regard this denial of childbearing as good or not. Children, surely, should not be regarded as a curse that prevents fulfilment of the person. For all the difficulty and pain involved in rearing children, they are almost universally regarded as a blessing, not a curse. How good or healthy is it to deny the physicality that makes us human?

There is, also, a strong class bias in the insistence that transcendence is possible for men but denied to women. A coal miner's son, or a factory worker's son, or an unemployed man's son in the time that de Beauvoir was writing would probably have been most amused to be told that he could look forward to being anything he wanted. Much the same observation could be made today. Freedom to have an undefined future is very much the privilege of the rich. It is not the universal condition of men, and only rich women are likely to benefit from this kind of opportunity—as both rich men and women could do before feminism, as well.

There are other ironies in the idea that a housewife, being denied fulfilment, *doing* nothing, can only glory in what she has.

First of all, careers outside the home in our materialistic society are generally aimed precisely at *having* more. Moreover, who says that the woman at home does nothing? On what rational grounds should the building of a home and the nurturing of relationships be regarded as 'nothing', whereas the building of a matchbox and the nurturing of a geranium be regarded as 'something'—just because they are performed as a job? Yes, housecleaning is boring and never conquered; yet this does not define its real nature or value. After all, much work outside the home is also boring and never conquered, as a garbage disposal worker could no doubt testify.

This dichotomy between immanence at home, with children and femininity, as opposed to transcendence out in the working world, with freedom and maleness, is quite ridiculous. Only the richest of men are able to make of their lives precisely what they want—and it certainly does not guarantee their happiness. Only the richest of women can share that privilege, no matter how many feminist laws are enacted. The rest of the world muddles along, living within the limitations that reality imposes, and are not all desperately unhappy as a result.

To be sure, oppression is never good. But take away oppression and what you have is not self-determination—it is more comfortable restriction. It is still restriction—as long as we are human, and mortal, and relational, we will never be absolutely free in the sense that de Beauvoir advocates; and pursuing it only brings frustration and loneliness. De Beauvoir's ultimate goal for any human is liberty. Yet the kind of liberty she proposes is literally impossible, for we are contingent beings in a finite universe. To aim for freedom as unlimited possibility is irrational, and as a basis for a social movement will inevitably conflict with reality sooner or later.

Simone de Beauvoir spells out what most feminist writing assumes—that the best thing a human being can have is freedom.

For Betty Friedan, it was freedom to have a career, not to be bound by home duties or the burden of child care. For Germaine Greer it was sexual freedom, without marriage and without conventional ideas of faithfulness or responsibility. Different feminists have concentrated on different aspects of these freedoms, but it was no accident that the movement began as women's *liberation*. It is a philosophy that has washed throughout Western society, with little thought for its deeper meaning. The insistence on personal freedom, to have no restriction on my self-expression, my sexuality, my lifestyle, my career choices, is probably the foremost ethic of the modern Western world.

The feminist argument is that men have throughout history had that freedom and denied it to women, so now we need to work to free women. Whether men have it is problematical, but whatever it is men have, that's what feminists want for women. However this presupposes another issue, which needs to be examined before we can determine whether this is a worthy goal. That is, is it true that what we want for men is exactly the same as what we want for women?

WHAT DOES IT MEAN TO BE 'WOMAN'?

Feminism has been the effort to make life better for women. From the start, there have been particular goals, such as abortion rights and child-care laws, but more generally it is a movement dedicated to improve the lot of women. This presupposes something very important—that feminists know what a 'woman' is. For until you have a theory of what a woman is, you don't know what's good for her.

What is a woman? She is a human being—but feminism is not a movement for human rights in general, it is a movement for the rights of women in particular. Woman is different from man; but how exactly? Until that is known, it is difficult to have any rational basis for activism.

So, how can we define 'woman'? This is a problem that has raged through feminist texts for decades. Of recent years, since feminism has entered the academy and its proponents have had the time for more precise discourse, a major debate has sprung up over this question 'what is woman?'. The debate is, in general terms, between the *essentialists* who think there is an answer to the question—that there is some way of defining 'woman', whatever that may be—and the *constructionists*, who argue that all such definitions have been political constructs designed to subjugate women.

Essentialism is a belief in true essence—that which is most irreducible, unchanging, and therefore basic to a person. In feminist theory, essentialism appears in a variety of ways. Most obviously, essentialism is seen in appeals to a pure or original femininity, a female essence, outside the boundaries of the social, and so untainted (though perhaps repressed) by a patriarchal order. Further, essentialism is fundamental to claims for the autonomy of a female voice. The whole activity of writing and discoursing within feminism, in fact, presumes that there is a thing that all this writing is about—woman. Feminism as an

It's that vexed question: do men and women behave differently because of differences in their upbringing, or because distinct, genetically programmed biological imperatives are unfolding?... Rogers... concludes in Sexing the Brain *that there is no proof that fetal hormones make any contribution to sex differences in human behaviour...Kimura reviews the same literature, only to find that the idea of biologically programmed sex differences in human ability is persuasive...Often, the authors draw opposite conclusions from the same findings.*

(NEW SCIENTIST REVIEW OF *SEXING THE BRAIN* BY LESLEY ROGERS AND *SEX AND COGNITION*, BY DOREEN KIMURA)

activity, then, must be essentialist.

Constructionism, defined in opposition to essentialism and concerned with its philosophical refutation, insists that essence is itself an historical construction. Constructionists take any 'essence' as the starting point for their own projects, and proceed to argue that previously assumed self-evident kinds (like 'man' or 'woman') are in fact merely the effects of political discussion. Constructionists are engaged in questioning the processes which work together to produce all seemingly 'natural' or 'given' objects. In short, constructionists reject the idea that any essential or natural givens precede the processes of social determination. Such feminists "challenge both dominant and most dissident accounts of identity by asserting that sexual identity cannot be viewed as fixed".[10]

The question boils down to the famous question: Is woman born or made? Historically, essentialism—that woman is born—has been very important. Part of the success of feminism has been that women have stood together and insisted: '*We* are women, but we are not what you say women are'. One classic example in feminist literature is the story of Sojourner Truth, a black woman who escaped slavery in the Southern States of the USA. The occasion was nothing to do with feminism; it was an anti-slavery rally in Indiana, at which white women and men had gathered. However as the rally began, a white male took the opportunity to speak against the idea of equal rights for women (for white women had insisted on taking part in the anti-slavery movement, wishing to speak at rallies just like this). This man's argument was that woman was too weak to perform her share of the stressful labour required—that she was innately the physical inferior to man. Sojourner immediately took the stage and bared

---

10. Chris Beasley, *What is Feminism, Anyway? Understanding Contemporary Feminist Thought*, Allen and Unwin, Sydney, 1999.

her breasts to prove that she was a woman, and listed the activities she had been forced to carry out as a slave. "That man over there say that women needs to be helped into carriages, and lifted ober ditches, and to have the best places…ain't I a woman? Look at me? Look at my arm!…I have plowed, and planted, and gathered into barns, and no man could head me—and ain't I a woman? I have borne five children and I seen em mos all sold off into slavery, and when I cried out with a mother's grief, none but Jesus hear—and ain't I a woman?"

Unlike most white women's rights advocates, Sojourner Truth could refer to her own personal life experience as evidence of woman's ability to be the work equal of man, to undergo persecution and physical abuse, and be a parent. Her story is still repeated often in polemical feminist works to drive home the point that women as a category are not essentially weak, dependent, and unable to compete with men. Similar arguments have been used all along the path of women's liberation. Are women denied equal pay because they cannot work as hard as men? Feminists insist they can work as hard. Are women kept at home because they are innately soft, motherly creatures? They are innately no such thing, say feminists; they are strong, and biology is not destiny. Whatever characteristics women have been given historically to keep them away from the male arena, feminists have retorted that those characteristics are not necessarily what is essential to being a woman; that on the contrary, women can be strong, tough, competitive and competent.

This kind of essentialism has played an important political role in the battle for women's rights; but of late, the constructionists have begun to dominate. That is, many writers now deny that there is anything essential to being a woman at all. Women as a category have no more in common than members of the working class have as a category; that is, only superficial things to do with lifestyle and attitudes shaped by being put into a particular social mould. But just as a working class person could be totally different if brought up in a different society, so could a woman. There is nothing, absolutely nothing, that makes a person essentially a woman. As one feminist writes:

> *The work of writers such as Butler challenges any stable sexual identity or idea about sexuality, let alone any belief in that identity as the foundation of a sexual politics. Rather than perceiving an unalterable intelligibility within the self and desire, there is a recognition of elasticity.*[11]

So are there still feminist essentialists? Yes, certainly; they can be found, for instance, in the 'earth mother' feminism, such as in the 1992 work *Women who Run with the Wolves*.[12] It is the earthy, folkloric vision of women, which rejects the straitjackets of thinness, fashion and career and instead focuses on inner being, a more natural lifestyle and rediscovery of women's traditions. It is often very attractive, and a relief from the battleground of activist feminism. But for all its attraction, it is criticized for the very things it promotes: the traditional essence of woman. In its emphasis on the distinctness of the female body and its reproductive experience, it is criticized for coming close to reinforcing patriarchal ideas of gender difference. Its lack of irony and resistance to objectivity, its sentimentalization of love and friendship, its non-intellectualism and use of poetics and metaphor, can be seen as obstacles to liberation. As soon as there are differences from men, especially a celebration of female differences, the fear arises that inequality will follow.

---

11. Chris Beasley, *What is Feminism, Anyway?.*, *op. cit.*, p. 99; J. Butler has published several works on gender and sexuality.
12. Clarissa Pinkola Estes, *Women who Run with the Wolves: Contacting the Power of the Wild Woman*, Rider, London, 1992.

There are other essentialists, of course; indeed, most of the more popular feminist writers appear to be essentialists, although this is not the main focus of their writings. After all, it is difficult not to be one. In an ordinary, commonsense world, which is what most popular feminism appeals to, how can you deny that women are different from men? That being a 'woman' is something that can be talked about? It is in these less rigorous works that essentialism can hide as an accepted common-sense observation and feeling, without having to be defended meticulously as it would in an academic paper.

The problem is, for all the unspoken acceptance of essentialism in popular feminism, there is very little said about what being a woman is. There is a lot said, on the other hand, about what a woman is not. And what a woman is not, is usually what men think a woman is. A very large part of the more popular feminist writing consists in refuting images or definitions of women put forward explicitly or implicitly by men.

In her most recent book, *The Whole Woman*, Germaine Greer devotes a whole chapter to the ways in which woman is medically and socially defined as anything which is not a man. Her examples are procedures such as sex-change operations. Her point is that there is—there has to be—more to being a woman than not being a man. Basically all a man needs to 'become' a woman is to have his genitals removed. There is no uterus and ovaries transplant; there is no need for the transsexual to be able to bear children. In reality, the transsexual is not a woman. He is a man suffering from self-mutilation. Why is he legally and socially accepted as a woman? "No-one", says Greer with justifiable indignation, "ever asked women if they recognized sex-change males as belonging to their sex or considered whether being obliged to accept MTF [male-to-female] transsexuals as women was at all damaging to their identity or self-esteem".[13]

---

13. Germaine Greer, *The Whole Woman*, Alfred A. Knopf, New York, 1999, p. 74.

The same could be said of men who do not have the operation, who merely dress as women, take a female name and are referred to as 'she'. What right have these men to take on a feminine pronoun? They are not women; they are extreme minority males.

Yet Greer is another who rejects certain classifications of what woman is—in this case, anything that is not man—but who does not actually have a positive definition with which to replace it. She acknowledges that the denigration of the earth mother feminists, "flat-footed, broad-hipped figures of fun", is a loss to feminism, but she does not go so far as to endorse this identification of womanhood. What is a woman? Even amongst those who want to acknowledge that she exists, we don't know who she is.

The fact is, without some outside reference point or authority, it is impossible to define 'man' or 'woman'. If materialists are right, and this world is all we have, then all we ultimately know about man and woman is what we can see—and that is male and female. These are animal categories. They apply to any creature with sexual reproduction.

But what do these categories tell us about 'man' and 'woman'? If we rely purely on animal realities to tell us what 'man' and 'woman' are, the result is confusion. There are too many conflicting examples. Male chimpanzees have harems of many females with whom they mate; so do goats and horses. Female spiders and praying mantis eat their husbands after (or even while) mating. Male seahorses incubate the eggs within their bodies. Female turtles leave their eggs to hatch and survive unguarded. Even amongst humans, what is biologically 'male' and 'female' is confusing; there is still little agreement on what is 'hardwired' into the brain and what is just cultural influence. In any case, how can we draw conclusions from a fact of nature? Women bear babies—so? Does this mean they should be primarily homemakers or that they should have nothing to do with rearing children because they've already contributed their share? Knowing brute biological facts does not help us much in saying how men and women ought to act. This is the traditional philosophical problem of the naturalistic fallacy—just knowing what *is* does not tell us what *ought* to be.

As Simone de Beauvoir pointed out so long ago, "it is not upon physiology that values can be based; rather, the facts of biology take on the values that the existent bestows upon them".[14] What we think of 'man' and 'woman' are values that we impose upon the biological categories; the biological values do not determine them. It is significant that we do *not* think of each other as merely 'male' or 'female'; we recognize that our relationships are more than purely biological, that we have standards and morality and ideas in our relationships. The categories 'man' and 'woman' are about how we relate to one another. They are about how we treat one another, how we think of ourselves in relation to the other. They are relational terms, not animal ones. They are dependent upon animal differences, but are much more than that. A female ape is female, but she is not a woman; being a woman is something unique to being human, to the relationships we have. 'Man' and 'woman' are about people of different sexes living together on this planet, different but moral and trying to work out how to respond to each other in dignity and respect.

Biology can tell us about male and female, but little about man and woman. Society is not a species. Its ways and customs cannot be deduced from biology. Yet once we move beyond biology, any conclusions we draw are bound to be confused and subjective. Women are meant to be stay-at-home mums—who says? Is that just your opinion? Women should have fulfilling careers—who says? Why is that more reasonable for a woman?

---

14. Simone de Beauvoir, *The Second Sex, op. cit.*, pp. 68-9.

THE PHILOSOPHICAL CONFUSION OF FEMINISM

Feminism has failed to find a coherent goal for women, because it has failed to define what a woman is, and has posited an impossible goal for humanity anyway. It is not good enough to say 'we fight for the rights of women', for who defines what those rights are? Who says that a woman's best life is this way or that way? How do they know?

If there is a philosophical basis to feminism, it is the ideal of the absolute autonomy of the self. Although this is rarely spelt out so painstakingly as Simone de Beauvoir did, it is an ideal we can discern in a wide range of feminist writings. The aim is for women to be *liberated*; to be freed, and to be allowed to be whatever they want to be. They are to become fully human, with the assumption being that to be fully human is to be fully free. However if that is what being fully human is, not only are we facing a very bleak future, but we must say that there have been very few (if any) 'full' humans ever born. For humans actually need each other, and like to be with each other. They are dependent on each other and develop relationships with each other. On the whole, humans do not aim to be fully free; they aim to be in harmony with other humans, helping and being helped. For women to try to be independent, to be free in this sense, is for women to be something impossible and hardly desirable. It is a philosophy that has left reality behind.

Moreover, the feminist philosophy fails to understand what a woman is. Both essentialist and constructionist ideas fail; either from being essentialist and therefore somehow demeaning, or constructionist and therefore, in the end, without meaning. Feminism is caught on the horns of a dilemma. Either women are essentially different from men, and the spectre of inequality arises; or the difference is a social construct, and therefore we don't know what 'woman' is any more.

If we can't say what a woman is; if we can't say what makes a woman's life good; if we can't even be clear on what is the aim of a human's life, how can we have a useful feminism? Feminist policies have in many cases gone notoriously wrong. Is it surprising, given the lack of ideas about what makes people's lives good? A movement that cannot even claim a coherent, workable philosophy is a movement that is ideologically bankrupt.

≈ Chapter 4 ≈

THE MORALITY
OF FEMINISM

Feminism is a profoundly moralistic movement. It is a system of ideas that not only states or argues for certain items of knowledge, or facts, but gives guidelines as to how to live. Although this may seem strange in our post-modern world where no one is supposed to tell us how we 'ought' to live, feminism is strongly directive as to what we ought to do. It insists that the personal and the political cannot be separated. Feminism is not just a matter of ordering public affairs; it is a way of life, a way of making decisions, something that will influence life choices and affect the basic values on which individual lives and society is run. In other words, it is a highly moral ideology.

Its claims are also very high—about 'justice' and 'rights' and other such lofty concepts. It takes the high moral ground, battling 'oppression' and 'subjugation'. Feminism purports to provide the 'right' way to live, to give values that will ensure justice for society and for individuals. Yet as a moral philosophy, feminism does not bear close examination. A brief look at its moral statements demonstrates that the 'right' way to live can be very confusing indeed.

It is difficult to find a consistent moral ground for the pronouncements of feminism. On what moral principle, for instance, should a feminist woman make decisions? How can it be decided that an action or a choice is morally allowable? It is certainly not on the basis that it will hurt no-one. Feminist decisions have hurt many people—husbands, children, and grandparents who no longer have access to their grandchildren, to name but some. Families cannot be dismantled without severe hurt on many counts, and feminism has unquestionably worked for the dismantling of family structures. According to feminism, this hurt may be justified, if the interests of the woman are served by her leaving.

Perhaps, then, the moral principle is: 'I must do what makes me happy'. A little selfish perhaps, but maybe justified given the downtrodden state of women. Yet this fails too, for feminism has demonstrably made women *un*happy. The lives of professional feminists are filled with pain. Erica Jong has had three failed marriages. Germaine Greer has been left grieving after repeated attempts at artificial insemination failed to provide her with a child. Phyllis Chesler, absolutely dedicated to the feminist cause, spent years in lonely isolation because in her illness none of her colleagues thought to visit her. She, like Marilyn French, has turned to a lesbian relationship simply because her relationships with men were so painful. Facing death, Marilyn French told one interviewer: "I don't expect very much from life, and I always expected everything and wanted everything and I wanted it all at once. That's not very realistic and it tends to make for unhappiness."[1]

Perhaps the individual pain of pioneers is a necessary price to pay in order to build a better and more equitable society. Perhaps the goal is the most happiness for the many, or justice for the majority. Perhaps the overriding goal, the moral principle of feminism, is to sacrifice anything for the sake of a society in which women are truly empowered and independent, and therefore happy. However, if feminism is meant to bring that kind of society, it can only be said to have dismally failed. The empowerment that feminism brings does not demonstrably lead to greater happiness. In many cases, it seems to have lead to greater *un*happiness.

It seems that feminism cannot give a consistent moral principle that will justify its recommended actions. Feminism wants 'freedom' yet has not, and cannot, provide a coherent view of what 'freedom' consists of. It wants 'justice' and yet consistently recommends courses of action that are palpably selfish and unjust. It wants happiness for women, yet is unable to agree on what a 'woman' is, let alone what would make for her happiness, and has

---

1. Marilyn French in Susan Mitchell (ed.), *Icons, Saints and Divas: Intimate Conversations with Women who Changed the World*, HarperCollins, Sydney, 1997, p. 162.

pursued an agenda that has led to widespread unhappiness.

Perhaps some light can be shed on this confusing moral land-scape by examining the most prominent and contentious moral issue raised by feminism in the last 30 years—abortion.

CASE STUDY: ABORTION

I had never delved into the particularities of the abortion debate until researching for this book, being neither Roman Catholic nor a 'Right-to-Lifer'. Like all controversial moral arguments, I have found the abortion debate to be plagued with 'hard-case' arguments. It is frequently difficult to get beyond such emotive episodes to genuine moral discussion. Yet let us for the moment consider this debate on rational terms, and see what a feminist position involves.

There are a range of reasons given for why abortion should be allowed. First and foremost, the mother's right to be in con-trol of her own body is asserted. Pregnancy is a major event in a woman's life, with overwhelming physical and psychological consequences, and it is her decision whether she is prepared to undergo this experience. No-one should be able to force her to undergo such a major change in her life.

This is the essence of one of the arguments used in the famous *Roe vs Wade* case in 1973, which brought legalized abor-tion into the United States and proved the watershed for many other countries. Sarah Weddington, plaintiff's attorney, argued that because of the impact of pregnancy, a mother should be able to choose whether or not to bring a pregnancy to term without having this choice circumscribed by the state. Pregnancy and child-rearing can impede women's access to careers, public life and economic freedom; indeed, they always have. Part of the struggle for equality for women must involve freedom from enforced childbirth. As feminist writer Judith Thomson insists:

> *If women are denied rights over their own bodies, they are denied rights to equal participation in the work of the world; if they are not permitted to make, for themselves, such deeply important decisions as whether to bear a child, they are not permitted to occupy the status of autonomous adult, morally equal to men.*[2]

This argument becomes more specific when the pregnancy is a result of rape or incest. These hard cases are frequently part of pro-abortion argument, for it hardly seems fair that the woman should undergo the second—perhaps life-long—trauma of having an unplanned and unwanted baby, after having just suffered the trauma of an illegal attack. The case is particularly strong when the 'woman' involved is a child. The stress, both emotional and physical, of the assault can be almost unbearable—what right has the state to impose the extra stress of pregnancy and childbirth? Only a woman who has been through such a terrible experience can know how bad it is.

Arguments concerning the well-being of the mother also insist that abortion must be available when the mother's life is in danger. Childbirth is dangerous; even with modern medical technology and knowledge, death in childbirth can happen. In this case, it is the medically sound and ethical practice to abort the child.

Another major argument for abortion is the tragedy of death from botched abortions. Where abortion is not legally available, it is argued, abortions nevertheless happen in large numbers, and the results can be horrific. Death, injury or infertility can arise from poor antisepsis and inexpert help. The figures quoted vary, but it is asserted that this is a serious social issue and that it is

---

2. Judith Jarvis Thomson, 'Abortion', *The Boston Review*, 20/3/99.

irresponsible of the state not to provide a safe medical procedure for those women who need to have abortions.

Another line of argument concerns the status of the foetus. Those who oppose abortion will often make statements such as 'abortion is murder'. Not so, argues the pro-abortion camp; for a foetus is not the same as a person. It may be a person-in-potentia, but before a certain stage it is simply a developing clump of cells. A fertilized egg does not have wants, hopes, fears, likes and dislikes; it does not experience pain or desire. It does not have mental activity. It may even divide to form more than one person. Very detailed embryology becomes involved in this aspect of the debate. There are arguments over 'viability'—the stage at which a baby can be said to be an independent person, capable of independent life outside the mother. Different groups choose different standards by which to declare the foetus or embryo a 'person', but the essential argument is that while in the womb, the child has not yet entered the human population.

Then, there is the argument on behalf of the child itself. It is unfair, even cruel, it is argued, to bring a child into the world if it cannot expect a reasonably happy life or level of care. A study from Scandinavia asserts that children born after their mothers are denied abortion face serious challenges. These children had a more insecure childhood, more delinquency, more psychiatric care, and more early marriages than did children in a comparison group.[3] A similar argument concerns babies who have a strong likelihood of being deformed or diseased in some way— something doctors are increasingly able to determine through testing in-utero. If a child is going to have a miserable life, pro-abortionists argue, it is not fair to let it be born.

A general argument is that even though pro-abortionists

---

3. David A. Grimes, 'The Continuing Need for Late Abortions', The Journal of the American Medical Association, 1998, 280, pp. 747-750.

cannot *prove* that the foetus has no right to life, neither can anti-abortionists *prove* that the foetus has a right to life. This is what Judith Thomson argued in a prominent article in the *Boston Review*. Therefore, she concluded, since neither side can prove its case, anti-abortionists have no right to impose their views on others. "What the supporters [of pro-life] want is a license to impose force; what the deniers want is a license to be free of it. It is the former that needs the justification."[4]

There are other arguments found in slogan form in pamphlets or on posters, such as "abortion is a fact of life", "no contraceptive is 100% effective"[5] and so on. Such statements are not meant to be considered arguments; but their emotive effect is powerful, and can be taken as factors in the pro-choice decision.

It is obvious that pro-abortionists find these arguments convincing. Why that is so is rather obscure. For despite the stridency of their demands, none of these arguments actually stand up to scrutiny. They may be emotionally powerful, but only at the cost of being illogical. Perhaps that is not regarded as important in such an emotive and personal issue. However for a movement that claims to have the moral right on its side, logic in its position would seem to be rather important.

1. A woman must have the right to control her own body
Take for instance the argument on behalf of the mother's right to

---

4.   Judith Jarvis Thomson, 'Abortion', *The Boston Review*, 20/3/99. Many of the arguments presented above are summarized in her paper; they can also be found in any standard feminist book that mentions abortion, or through the hundreds of web sites found through a search on 'abortion'. One place to start is the National Organization for Women homepage, www.now.org.
5.   Taken from 'Facts about Abortion', a Children by Choice pamphlet (Children by Choice Association, Queensland).

A baby girl lived for 80 minutes after medical staff tried to abort her, Darwin Coroners Court heard yesterday. Baby J was alive when born at about five months after her mother underwent an induced procedure to cause a termination, but died after receiving no medical treatment, the court heard. Counsel assisting the coroner, Peter Barr, told the court Baby J showed clear signs of life when she was checked by a nurse after delivery at Darwin Private Hospital on July 14 last year. "She cried, she moved, she was breathing independently and she had an obvious heartbeat". But Mr Barr said the baby was not given a medical assessment and remained in the delivery suite for 80 minutes until she died. Northern Territory coroner Greg Cavanagh heard Baby J was healthy for her gestation period. Mr Cavanagh said the baby was capable of feeling pain, but nothing was done to assess or otherwise care for her. Kai Man Henry Cho, Department of Obstetrics and Gynaecology director at Royal Darwin Hospital, told the court he had interviewed the 20-year-old mother of Baby J. He said she had a career in the defence forces and said she could not cope with a child.

(THE AUSTRALIAN, 3/11/99)

autonomy, to control of her body and her life. Pregnancy certainly is a major event in a woman's life. It does have a life-changing impact. Why, however, is that any grounds for allowing abortion? First of all, if the state—as the body of people—for whatever reason thinks killing foetuses is wrong, then the state will restrict whoever is doing it. The state restricts all sorts of behaviour. It restricts us from driving too fast. It forces us to go to school. It even restricts behaviour which may have a compelling motivation: the impact of poverty on a person can be life-threatening, but the state nonetheless restricts activities such as theft.

In any case, consider what this argument is saying about people's rights. Essentially, this argument implies, the baby doesn't have the right to impose upon its mother. Apart from the fact that the baby has no choice in this matter, what if a murdering husband made this claim? What if he claimed that he murdered his wife because she imposed upon his freedom? "This woman profoundly changed my life and I didn't want her to do that." Does this allow children to kill their parents? Parents hugely change children's physiology and life choices—does that give the children the right to dispose of their parents?

In any case, how can we have a right of personal autonomy when we have sexual reproduction? It is physiologically impossible. The state does not burden women against their will; the baby does. The state is merely saying that restoring personal autonomy at the cost of someone's life is not legal. In any case, every woman (except those who are raped, or the very small percentage who experience contraceptive failure) *has* control over her own body. She has, in fact, two opportunities to choose whether or not to have children. She has a choice of whether to have sex or not, and another choice in whether to use contraceptives or not. If a woman has ignored these choices, what right does she have to demand a third go at the cost of another's life?

There are alternatives to abortion for an unwanted pregnancy. An initial alternative is prevention; to teach the reality of the consequences of sex and the responsibility to practise it wisely (which means not just with a condom, but in a situation where pregnancy need not be a disaster[6]). Once the pregnancy

---

6. Another matter, not to be discussed here, is how much the feminist movement may have contributed to the sexual revolution, which has led to so many women suffering from poorly planned sex and poor sexual relationships. For a history of the sexual revolution, see Tony Payne and Phillip D. Jensen, *Pure Sex*, Matthias Media, Sydney, 1998.

happens, there are options of adoption—with adequate support for the emotional and physical needs of the mother—or of helping the mother keep and raise the child.

Pregnancy may be uncomfortable, and a woman might not want to go through with it.[7] Adoption is traumatic for the mother. Yet there is hardly any valid morality in arguing that the death of a child is better than non-fatal inconvenience to the mother; and if as much effort and money were put into simplifying and supporting an option such as adoption, its attractiveness could improve no end—and provide a far more moral alternative to the death of the baby. If the mother does not want a baby, for whatever reason (such as those listed in the survey above), there are plenty of mothers who do. There is so much desire for adoptive children that the age limit for parents has recently been raised, and parents look overseas for longed-for children. The number of adoptions of overseas children in Australia was nearly twice as many as for local children in 1988-89.[8] Moreover, there is now little social stigma to being a single mother or to having a child out of wedlock. Illegitimacy does not exist as a legal category any more. Yet at a time where there is no such thing as an unwanted child in Australia, and single parenthood is accepted and even encouraged, we have thousands of abortions each year. The reasons are not adding up yet.

2. A victim of rape should have access to abortion
Rape and incest create appalling situations. There is no denying the suffering involved. The first point to be made, however, is that the slogan 'hard cases make bad laws' is true. If the law is to be just, it must be decided upon reasonable grounds, not emotional ones, however emotional we may feel. We will simply end up trad-

---

7. An argument used by Judith Thomson in the article mentioned above.
8. 'Adoptions Australia 1998-99', Australian Institute of Health and Welfare.

ing one 'hard case' for another. You have a 12-year-old raped by her father? I have a baby girl left to die in pain. Both are awful. Neither is a basis for law that covers all cases.

Moreover, apart from the fact that the crime committed on the mother is hardly the baby's fault, the abortion freedom being fought for is far wider than this limited group. Abortion is claimed as every woman's right, not just those who have been raped. If abortion is a fundamental right of every woman, then that is the case whether she has been raped or not. The argument does not match what is actually being argued for. It is quite possible that an anti-abortion law could contain room for hard cases on a case-by-case basis. However this is not good enough, as was seen in the 1998 debate over anti-abortion laws in Western Australia. The law already included provisions for abortion to be possible in hard cases, such as if the mother's life was in danger. This law was overturned

Dallas, Friday: Norma McCorvey, whose fight for the right to an abortion led to the landmark 1973 Supreme Court ruling in Roe v Wade, has changed her mind and joined the anti-abortion forces. Ms McCorvey, who was known as "Jane Roe" in the case, made the announcement on a Dallas radio station. She had since quit her job as a marketing director at A Choice for Women, *a gynaecological clinic operated by abortion-rights supporters, according to a staff member...* In an interview on the radio station WBAP, Ms McCorvey announced: "I'm pro-life. I think I have always been pro-life, I just didn't know it."
(SYDNEY MORNING HERALD, 12/8/95. Ms MCCORVEY NEVER HAD AN ABORTION.)

nonetheless, introducing the most liberal abortion laws in the nation, allowing abortion on informed consent of the mother.[9]

---

9. The Western Australian Parliament voted to legalize abortion on 2nd April 1998.

There are, sadly, some cases where the mother's life is somehow in conflict with the baby's life. If a pregnant woman has cancer, her chemotherapy, which is necessary to save her own life, may kill the foetus. This creates the need for a terrible decision, but sometimes one life does have to be chosen over another. Some mothers in this situation have chosen to save the baby at the cost of their own life; sometimes the alternate decision must be made. This is a terrible situation, and should not be used casually as an argument for abortion on demand. It is not the norm by any means.

It is hard not to conclude that the rape or life-in-danger argument is a red herring, included for its strong emotive appeal, even though most actual abortions taking place are nothing of the sort. A survey of women having abortions in New South Wales in 1992—a survey quoted by the pro-abortion group Children by Choice—showed that while most women had more than one reason for terminating the pregnancy, none of the abortions performed were for reasons of rape or incest. 60% gave reasons to do with not being able to afford a baby; 38% cited the potential for unwanted changes in lifestyle; 29% did not want to be a single mother; 25% felt they were too young; 27% wanted to establish their careers before having a child; 22% believed they should be married before having a child. Other reasons included partners or parents not wanting the woman to have a baby, not wanting children, not wanting others to know of the pregnancy, having enough children already, and 5% cited health reasons such as high blood pressure.[10]

It is impossible to deny that this is what abortion is really

---

10. 'Abortion: Women's reasons', a Children by Choice pamphlet, citing Pamela L. Adelson, Michael S. Frommer and Edith Wiesberg, 'A survey of women seeking termination of pregnancy in New South Wales', *The Medical Journal of Australia*, 1995, *163*, pp. 419-422.

about in our society—women having abortions, not because their lives are in danger, nor because they have been raped, but because a baby would be inconvenient. Yet high-profile abortion stories are about the hard cases, not the real cases. If we actually faced the reality of babies being aborted for the sake of convenience, we might not be so easily convinced.

3. Making abortion illegal causes suffering through back-yard abortions
It is hard to avoid a similar response to the 'death by botched abortion' argument. Yes, women have problems when they try to abort without expert help. How does that make legalized abortion valid? There are any number of other things which can be difficult to do without medical help—committing suicide, murdering, pulling out a rotten tooth. Which ones we decide to offer help for and which ones we don't has nothing to do with the difficulty of performing them. It has to do with whether the activity is a moral one. The argument that the procedure is dangerous in itself without medical help is irrelevant.

A *valid* moral argument from botched abortions would be that we should find some way to avoid the need for the abortion; just as a valid moral argument from the number of botched suicides would not be to make suicide easier, but to try to help people stop wanting it.

4. A foetus is not a viable life, or a real person
Our next kind of argument concerned the nature of the offspring. Much ink has been spilt over determining when a foetus becomes 'viable', at what point an embryo becomes a foetus and so on, to defend the non-personhood of the offspring. This seems rather to miss the point: when you're pregnant, the thing that follows is to have a baby. The 'line' is impossible to draw, as is demonstrated by the many different criteria suggested for drawing it. At any point from conception onwards, the fertilized egg is developing into a

*I was outspoken about a woman's
right to have an abortion—
yet I kept my own a secret from
everyone except a few friends.
I faced total confusion—this great
decision I'd made was exactly
aligned with feminist ideology;
yet my heart was broken and
I was emotionally destitute. I had
destroyed a life—a life which
I knew would have looked just
like my two living sons. I could
hardly breathe for the anger and
disgust which rose; I was not
worth the air I breathed.*

('MARION', IN MELINDA
TANKARD REIST, *GIVING SORROW
WORDS: WOMEN'S STORIES
OF GRIEF AFTER ABORTION*)

child. That child is a different
organism from the mother, with
different DNA; it is not part of the
mother's body. It will remain
dependent upon the mother (or
some other carer) up to 10 years of
age in some ways; up to 18 years in
others. There is no discrete point in
all that time which differentiates
between 'non-personhood' and
'personhood'. The line is arbitrary.

*5. It is cruel to bring an unwanted or
disabled child into the world*
What are we to make of the arguments which involve the future life
of the child? Is it unfair to bring a
child into the world if it is
unwanted or will have a miserable
life? We have already established
that no child need be unwanted, if
adoption is taken seriously. The
argument is, then, that these potentially unhappy children would be
better off dead. One questions the morality of this argument. The
future of a child is not determined; who are we to judge that a life
will be happy or unhappy? In any case, who are we to say that an
unhappy life is worse than no life at all? In this argument, more
than any other, we see the amoral arrogance of the pro-abortionist
position. Totally opposed to anything that will interfere in the life
of the mother, advocates will yet be the judge of a person's entire
life and deprive her of it if that life seems somehow deficient.

6. You must first prove that a foetus has a right to life
So we come to a peculiarly abstract argument for the availability of
abortion: Judith Thomson's claim that even though pro-abortionists cannot *prove* that the foetus has no right to life, neither can
anti-abortionists *prove* that the foetus has a right to life. "What the
supporters [of pro-life] want is a license to impose force; what the
deniers want is a license to be free of it. It is the former that needs
the justification."[11] In other words, the anti-abortionists want to
force a woman to have a child; the pro-abortionists want to be free
of that constriction; therefore, in a free society, those who want to
impose force need a thoroughly convincing justification for it. One
which, Thompson states, they don't have.

There are two issues here: whether anti-abortionists can
prove a right to life, and whether the onus is on them to do so.
In both cases, Thompson is playing semantics. So no one can
'prove', through reason alone, that the foetus has a right to life?
No, indeed; no one can prove that *any* person has a right to life.
Yet if anyone does, then we have no particular reason to say that
a foetus does not; as we saw, any dividing line is arbitrary. If
Judith Thompson believes she has a right to life, on what
grounds does she deny it to the foetus? It is the pro-abortionists
who have the burden of proof; that at some point, the foetus
moves from 'non-right' to 'right'. As we have seen, this could be
any time from conception to one year or onwards.

The second point is equally convoluted. In a free society,
Thompson argues, those who want to enforce something are the
ones who need to provide compelling reasons for doing so; otherwise they have no right to restrict the freedom of others. But who

---

11. Judith Thomson, 'Abortion', *op. cit.*

says it is the anti-abortionists who are doing the forcing? They just want a natural process to continue unhampered. It is the abortionists who are proving a restriction—a rather severe one, that removes the pregnancy altogether. If anyone needs to prove their case, surely it is the pro-abortionists who are proposing terminating what has traditionally been thought to be a life. Even if we can't *prove* that a foetus is a person, surely we should give it the benefit of the doubt rather than kill it outright. Semantic plays such as this prove nothing about right or wrong. In the absence of a coherent moral argument, they merely buy time.

We have yet to find a good argument for why abortion should be easily available. Perhaps we just haven't come across the right arguments yet. Maybe there is still a good argument to be found, so why worry? 'Right to life' can be dismissed as religious bias. However, even if the mother's rights are regarded as absolute and the child a non-person until birth, there are still very good reasons to question the proliferation of abortion clinics and the huge increases in abortion rates of recent years. A feminist whose only concerns are for the mother has good reason to protest against legalized abortion.

Consider, for example, the amount of money to be made out of abortion. Make no mistake, this is big business, and a big business generally run by men. Men are making money out of the discomfort of women. In Australia, abortions can cost up to $350. An estimated 80,000 Australian women each year have abortions.[12] That

---

12. These are the figures quoted by Children by Choice. The NSW Right to Life Association puts the figure at 100 000 per year. I have not been able to obtain official figures; no doubt they are difficult to ascertain since abortion is still technically illegal in most states. I have read figures of 190 per week and 10 000 per year for Western Australia. Most pro-abortionist literature claims that numbers are probably underestimated.

is 28 million dollars a year just on abortion costs; this is in addition to any post-abortion counselling or medical attention. Someone is making a lot of money. The huge amounts of money to be made from abortion would suggest, even to the minimally cynical, that there might be more than pure ideology involved in the push to have abortion easily available. Yet for some reason, this aspect fails to be investigated or publicized at all. If women were subjected to a barrage of advertising, counselling and the weight of public opinion to have some other invasive, uncomfortable and psychologically damaging procedure, surely this would be a matter of feminist outrage. Yet in the case of abortion, it is not.

But perhaps abortion has no negative psychological effects (to the mother, at least). Perhaps it genuinely is a safe, harmless procedure. The Council for Choice would have us believe so— "the unanimous consensus is that abortion does not cause negative psychological effects". A very little research, however, elicits numbers of papers which explore the potential for negative psychological effects following abortion.[13] There is hardly unanimous consent; enough people are concerned that numerous studies are still being carried out. In the meantime, a procedure which is at least of highly debatable psychological effect continues not only to be recommended for women, but fought for.

---

13. For instance, B. Major and R. H. Gramzow, 'Abortion as stigma: cognitive and emotional implications of concealment', *Journal of Personality and Social Psychology*, 1999, *77*, pp. 735-45; Catherine Cozzarelli, Nebi Sumer and Brenda Major, 'Mental models of attachment and coping with abortion', *Journal of Personality and Social Psychology*, 1998, *74*, pp. 453-467; G. Kam Congleton, Lawrence G. Calhoun, 'Post-abortion perceptions: a comparison of self-identified distressed and non-distressed populations', *International Journal of Social Psychiatry*, 1993, *39*, pp. 255-265; Catherine A. Barnard, 'The long-term psychosocial effects of abortion', *Dissertation Abstracts International*, 1991, *51*, p. 4038; P. Mueller and B. Major, 'Self-blame, self-efficacy and adjustment to abortion', *Journal of Personality and Social Psychology*, 1989, *57*, pp. 1059-1068.

Moreover, the wide availability of abortion leads directly to a very real possibility: women being forced to have abortions they do not want. This happens openly in China. In our more 'liberal' Western countries, it certainly happens, but with less honest acknowledgement. Consider the study quoted earlier about reasons for abortion in New South Wales: 12% of respondents gave as their reason partners not wanting the woman to have a baby, and for 6% the reason was that parents did not want the woman to have a baby. These are frightening figures, suggesting a coercion of women who have abortions not because they want to, but because others push them into it.[14]

I write this with a feeling of distinct puzzlement. I assumed before investigation that the abortion debate was at least a validly contentious moral issue with reasonable people doing the best they could to find reasonable moral conclusions. What I found instead is a confusing mixture of blind dogmatism and careful avoiding of the issue. Abortion debates, as far as I can tell as an outsider, very quickly descend into the emotional. Seeing the paucity of logic on the feminist side, I can understand why. The peculiar thing is why so many women have decided that this illogical and untenable moral position makes sense. We are not talking about women who have suffered the trauma of rape, or incest; there are not 80,000 of them turning up to abortion clinics in Australia each year. These are ordinary women, often married, frequently with other children, who simply decide that this is not the time for a baby— and that it is morally justifiable to terminate the baby's life. The baby, being inconvenient, can be killed. Somewhere along the line, thousands of women have been deluded into a morally indefensible position. They and their children are paying the price.

---

14. 'Abortion: Women's reasons', *op. cit.*

A MORAL PHILOSOPHY?

The feminist position insists that abortion is absolutely, fundamentally, a woman's right. A rather peculiar right it is, that allows women of one age to extinguish the life of women of another age. There is a rather deafening silence about the rights of an unborn woman to choose a fulfilled life. Yet why should abortion be such a fundamental right? What precisely is it that suits the feminist agenda, that makes feminists ignore so many of its detrimental effects for women? Abortion is necessary for "liberation" for it brings women that much closer to being without moral responsibility at all—able to have irresponsible sex with (almost) impunity. This tells us something about feminism, not about abortion. It tells us that the liberation that feminism wants is the freedom to be the same as the most irresponsible of men. It is the freedom to be utterly self-centred and to sacrifice others for one's own convenience and comfort—the very accusation that feminists have thrown against men.

Yet why should we be surprised that the morality of feminism is so utterly selfish? As we have seen, it is based on a philosophy that says the ultimate goal for any human being is complete and utter freedom from any constraint. This naturally appeals to our innate selfishness, which is perhaps why its arguments have gained such an eager hearing despite their logical flaws. If our goal is complete freedom, then we need to be able to dispense with uncomfortable restrictions—and a child is, certainly, a restriction. The child's rights are ignored in the feminist position on abortion because the philosophy teaches that the only person who matters is oneself; complete self-determination is the ultimate good.

In the end, the only coherent moral position that can arise from a philosophy of absolute freedom is selfishness—the pursuit of what I perceive to be my good, at the expense of all others. Husband, parents, and children are not as important as my right to self-determination. We have now reached the point of the ultimate sanction—extinguishing life that threatens my happiness.

The ethics of feminism are riddled with contradictions, for its basis is self-centredness and that is profoundly irrational. We are a social species; our survival is dependent upon our cooperation. No-one in our feminist, Western society is or can be independent. No-one forages all their own food, builds their own shelter, manufactures their own clothes. We need each other. We do not live alone, and a morality that ignores that principle simply will not work.

═ *Chapter 5* ═

FEMINIST HISTORY

We all take to selfishness like ducks to water, so it is not surprising that feminism would have seemed initially very attractive. However this movement is not just a passing fad; it has achieved academic respectability. If feminism is so bad, why has it prospered? Isn't it rather unlikely that so many women thinking seriously about their lives would be taken in by a fundamentally flawed movement? Not necessarily—especially since the mythology of feminism has incorporated within it a long and venerable history of important human rights achievements.

History is important to feminism because it establishes it not as a recent, radical movement but one with a long and honourable pedigree. Women's groups of the nineteenth century accomplished many worthy goals, and feminism benefits from being aligned with these groups. It gives feminism a legitimacy and a tradition and a place in history. It is also a good starting point for any polemical feminist book. Look how far we've come, feminist texts can say; look what we've accomplished and what we've had to fight against. Let's keep the anger alive; let's keep the movement going.

As one work has put it, "The introduction of Women's Studies in the 1970s really helped spread the knowledge of women's contributions through history".[1] There is a standard history of feminism, which usually begins in the late eighteenth century. Certain female novelists began writing careers at that time, and in essence created the literary form of the novel. Also significant was the French revolution, in which women took a large part, even though they were not granted citizenship rights after the revolution. Also in the late eighteenth century, the writer Mary Wollstonecroft wrote her famous *Vindication of the Rights of Women*, one of the classic feminist texts.

---

1. Sophie Grillet, *Feminism for Teenagers*, Piccadilly Press, London, 1997, p. 28.

The story then moves to the nineteenth century, with efforts to improve schooling for girls. Around the middle of the nineteenth century, certain women's groups in England became very active, campaigning on a range of social issues including the opportunity for single women to work, opening universities to women, the right of women to be trained as doctors, the right to vote, and moral issues such as prostitution. In America, many women were involved in the movement to end slavery, and then moved on to campaigning for the vote. By the time of the First World War, most of the battles had been more or less won; women had the vote and access to education and work; and 'First-Wave' feminism, as it is called, is considered to have ended.[2]

History is never simple. Any short history inevitably smooths over historical subtleties and gives only one perspective on what happened. That is part of the nature of writing history, and as long as the author does her best to indicate where selective use of data is taking place and to give a fair coverage, this need not be a major problem. However, too often feminist histories go beyond the basic problems of history to outright distortions. Sometimes, putting only one point of view so distorts the picture that what is left is hardly history at all.

It is not that every feminist history is a fabrication of lies. However in researching feminism, I have found in the standard feminist histories generalizations that misrepresent the period, one-sided accounts without historical context, and plain mistakes. The story, repeated in feminist texts and introductory works, is very unfair to the women who fought social battles in the nineteenth century. Modern feminism claims continuity

---

2. Feminist histories of nineteenth-century England can be found in books such as Philippa Levine, *Victorian Feminism 1850-1900*, Hutchinson, London 1987; Barbara Caine, *English Feminism 1780-1980*, Oxford University Press 1997; Olive Banks, *Becoming a Feminist: The Social Origins of 'First Wave' Feminism*, Wheatsheaf Books, Brighton, 1986.

with a tradition that is, in truth, not theirs. They write their own views into the battles of the past, even though the battles were on quite different grounds. Nineteenth-century history does not give us a picture of a long, victorious struggle of women against oppression. Women struggled, certainly; but so did men, and together they worked to right social wrongs, usually for very different reasons from those which modern feminists hold dear.[3]

This chapter is not an effort to rewrite women's history. That worthy task is far beyond the scope of this book. In what follows, however, we will examine some of the episodes of standard feminist history, and insert some question marks where they are necessary. We will look at four major struggles of English feminist history: women's education, women's work, votes for women, and the fight against prostitution laws.

These particular struggles matter because in claiming these victories feminism has enormous emotional pull over women. The standard view makes it very difficult for women to reject or even criticize feminism. Despite the glaring problems, the unspoken (or spoken) retort is always: "How can you criticize feminism? If it were not for feminists, you would not be at university/have a job/ be able to vote". Yet this is an unfair retort, and one that does not accurately reflect how these social changes came about. In this brief overview, we will start to see where an alternative explanation might be necessary.

EDUCATION FOR WOMEN

The 1840s saw increased energy given to educating women.

---

3. This tendency can also be seen in modern film versions of old novels. Consider, for example, the feminist values read into such works as Jane Austen's *Mansfield Park* or Louisa May Alcott's *Little Women*.

Many girls' schools were already in existence, but they mostly taught 'accomplishments'—sketching, deportment, the things a lady needed to know in order to act as a lady. There was very little education of the mind, or imparting of intellectual information. Some of the new education was designed to help women become better wives and mothers, to be able to converse more easily with their husbands, and to be able to teach children. Working-class girls were trained in domestics. There was some effort for individual women to give 'lectures for working women' in the evenings.

There were some with more ambitious ideals for women: the entrance to university. One of the biggest obstacles was that the universities refused to let women even attempt their admission examinations. It took a great deal of persuasion before Cambridge was the first to be pushed into letting girls take its exams in 1863, and the results (in which the girls did very well in everything other than arithmetic) were highly influential.

This struggle is usually taken to be a major feminist victory—women triumphing over the men who would keep them in subjection. Yet a few qualifying observations are necessary. Strides were made in education throughout all society. The 1870 Education Act for England created public schooling for children of all classes and both sexes. While activist women were giving evening lectures, male radicals were doing the same for working-class men.

It is true that women were excluded from higher education before this time. However, so were by far the majority of citizens. University education was not the entry to life and professional work that it is now; it was an elite finishing-school for upper-class young men. The actual education they received could be absolutely minimal. It was a matter of social status for rich men's sons. There was no real examination for a degree in Oxford until 1800. Opinions as to the value of a degree could be fairly scathing. Oxford scholar Mark Pattison remarked that the letters B.A. have only a social value. "They are an evidence that a youth has been able to afford not only the money, but...the time, to live three years among gentlemen, doing nothing, as a gentleman should".[4] The academic fellows were not allowed to marry, and had to be ordained; their life was more monastic than academic. No one who was not a member of the Church of England could take a degree before 1858; in 1871 all religious tests were abolished. In 1863 students who were not members of a college were admitted to Oxford and in 1869 to Cambridge. It was at this time—1869—that the first women's college was established, followed by four more before 1893.

In fact, the pitiful state of the universities with their low level of academic endeavour, the sinecure they offered to teachers, and their exclusivity, prompted a powerful wave of university reform in the second half of the nineteenth century. The system of university education was overhauled, in which admitting women to university was a part. Moves were also made to allow poor students to get a university education. Up until this time, anyone who was not a member of the upper-class was effectively excluded from attending university. (Thomas Hardy's novel *Jude the Obscure* narrates a working man's struggle to enter university.) London University, officially created in 1836 (although it was not allowed to confer degrees to all its students until 1858) was established to help students who were excluded from Oxford and Cambridge for religious reasons or through poverty. It admitted women to degrees from 1878. The University of Durham was also founded for students of limited means by an

---

4. Mark Pattison, 1868; quoted in Owen Chadwick, *The Victorian Church*, Adam and Charles Black, London, 1970, p. 442. For the state of universities also see such works as G. M. Trevelyan, *British History in the Nineteenth Century and After (1782-1919)*, Penguin Books, Harmondsworth, 1965; or other standard histories of the nineteenth century.

act of parliament in 1832. There was another burst of university founding later in the century in Manchester, Leeds, and Bristol, and a number of other sites across England.

Many people, not just women's groups, had been concerned about the medieval nature of the universities. Two Royal Commissions in 1858 and 1877 investigated the universities and recommended drastic changes. The professoriate was increased and re-endowed so that it became a resident, university body. Uniform regulations were enforced for the selection and salaries of professors, and fellowships were thrown open to merit.

Women's access to education was an important social change. However to treat it as essentially a female struggle against male domination, without consideration of the major changes education underwent in the nineteenth century, is to distort what happened. Not only did the nature of education change, but the availability of education for a whole range of social groups became possible, and all required struggles against long-held prejudices.

WOMEN'S WORK

Another major issue for feminist history is women's right to work. In 1859, a Society for the Promotion of the Employment of Women was established. At first, the campaigns of the 1850s and 1860s assumed that employment was only a problem for single women; the issue of married women working never arose. To a large extent, this was driven by circumstances. For several reasons, there was a significant rise in the numbers of middle-class women who did not have the opportunity to get married. At the same time, middle-class families were less and less inclined to support these 'parasitical' sisters and daughters. The numbers of women competing for a limited number of eligible jobs (mostly as governesses) were increasing. The campaigners in the fight for employment were concerned with better educating women to make them more employable, and to combat prejudices against women working. In practice, the fight was on behalf of middle-class women.

The practical results of the campaign remained small, but set a great theoretical change in motion by bringing the idea forward that paid work offers dignity and fulfilment which the single and unwanted Victorian lady could not otherwise have. Part of the problem was the opinion that it was somehow degrading for women to accept money for work. There was evidently something morally noble about their volunteer status.[5] Both women looking for work, and the campaigners on their behalf, suffered severe antagonism. They had strong opponents in male employees and all-male unions.

There was also an ideology against them, that kept women in the home, and moreover devalued what they did there. Before the industrial revolution, home-based industry meant that women were part of the family business, and there was no necessary clash between homemaking and productive work. The industrial revolution, however, pulled work out of the home. Work was now at the factory, or the office. The productive work, which brought in money and was thus seen as valuable, was that done by men outside the home.

By the end of the century, however, women had won the right to employment in a range of public service jobs, and the first women were beginning to take up professions such as medicine. The fight required considerable effort, breaking down social barriers and changing assumptions about women's capabilities and their place in the world. Women were able to conquer the public

---

5.   In fact, this is an example of the very different values attached to work in nineteenth-century Britain. Amateur 'work', be it for charity, science or in sport, was considered in many ways more important or valuable than paid work.

arena, and insist that they were capable of valuable, productive work, and that it was not just men who could or should participate in public life. Again, this has been seen as a win for feminism, fighting for women's rights against the men who would keep them poor and dependent in the home.

Yet once again, the story is far more complicated than this. Women had always worked outside the home, both before and after the industrial revolution. The woman worker, married or unmarried, existed long before the advent of industrial capitalism, earning her keep as a spinner, dressmaker, goldsmith, brewer, metal polisher, buttonmaker, lacemaker, nursemaid, dairymaid, or houseservant. What is more, women's work before the industrial revolution was not all home-based industry combined with family care. Women sold goods at markets, were traders and itinerant peddlers, hired themselves out as casual labourers, nurses or laundresses, made pottery, silk, lace, clothing, metal goods and hardware, wove cloth and printed calico in workshops, and if necessary, sent their children to wet nurses or others. Most workers were young and single, working away from their own homes; but married women would have various locations of work, and the time spent on domestic tasks varied depending on the pressures of work and the economic circumstances.[6]

This description is also true of the nineteenth century. The female workforce remained mostly young and single, in domestic service or textile manufacturing, and married women also

---

6. See for instance G, M Trevelyan, *British History in the Nineteenth Century and After: 1782-1919*, Penguin Books, Harmondsworth, 1965, p. 21; and Joan W. Scott 'The Woman Worker' in *A History of Women in the West*, Vol 4: Emerging Feminism from Revolution to World War, Genevieve Frasse and Michelle Perrot (eds), The Belknap Press of Harvard University Press, Cambridge, Massachusetts and London, England, 1993, p. 399.

worked in textile factories. The textile industry was not the major employer of women; more worked in markets, shops, laundry, keeping boarding houses, making matches, artificial flowers and jewellery. Many women had a whole range of jobs. Needlework, always women's work, expanded as the clothing trades grew, providing steady employment for some women and a fall-back for others. Farming trades were many but poorly paid.

Yet middle-class ladies did not want this kind of work. The surplus of single women who did not have the opportunity to marry, desperately needed work to survive. On the whole, however, they were only interested in 'genteel' jobs such as being a governess to rich people's children. The fight to enable women to work was actually the fight to enable middle-class women to avoid trades or retail. It may well be a good thing that women took up professions; certainly having women in areas such as medicine is desirable when half of patients are female. However, to couch the entire struggle in terms of 'women's rights' against oppressive men is not to tell the whole story. It ignores the struggle against middle-class prejudice. It also ignores the fights waged by middle and working-class women to help working-class women out of the factories, where they and their children were dreadfully exploited. Paid work in nineteenth-century Britain was hardly something all women considered beneficial. The issue of women and work in industrial Britain is a very complicated one.

The feminist picture also ignores the differences among men's work experience, which could be interrupted and irregular. Men worked under appalling conditions in coalmines at very low pay. Men could be press-ganged into virtual slavery in the Navy.[7] At the same time, there were some women who held permanent positions in craft industries. It is simply not true that

---

7. If captains of the Royal Navy had trouble hiring enough hands for their ships, they were allowed to kidnap able-bodied men and force them into service.

men had all the (good) work and would not let women have it. Working conditions over the whole country were forced to change during the nineteenth century, not just with industrialization but also with population: the population of England and Wales increased by some five million between 1851 and 1871. Exports rose from 71 million pounds in 1850 to nearly 200 million pounds in 1870. Society had to adjust to massive changes.[8]

There was considerable struggle on the part of various philanthropic groups in nineteenth-century England to help those who were displaced by the widespread changes in English society throughout that century. Many women struggled with the new culture, just as many others appreciated and benefited from the changes in technology and wealth. Single women who fought to be allowed to earn a living in the kind of jobs they liked made up one such struggle in a confusing context.

SUFFRAGETTES AND THE VOTE

The best known and best documented aspect of nineteenth-century women's movements was the fight for the vote. It was also the most drawn-out campaign; the first writings in favour of the female vote were in the 1820s, an organized campaign began in the 1860s, and victory was finally achieved in 1928. Interestingly, the vote was not claimed by women as an abstract and inalienable right. Rather it was argued that since Britain claimed to be a nation of representative government, women should not be denied that representation. Also, the ground of women's moral purity was used. Women, it was claimed, would influence parliament to make morally right decisions (an interesting comment on their opinion of politicians).

---

8. David Thomas, *England in the Nineteenth Century: 1815-1914*, Penguin Books, Hamondsworth, 1950.

The fight became vicious as it dragged on, involving hunger strikers, rocks thrown at speakers, and one famous suicide when the militant suffragette Emily Davidson threw herself in front of the horses in the Derby race of 1913.

As we know, the vote was finally won, and again women proved they were not to be held back by misogynist men denying them their rights. Yet once again, the battle was not just about gender, and it was not all one-way. While the national battle for the vote went on, women were making great strides in local government. In 1869, single rate-paying women were granted the vote at a municipal level and made use of it. Women had a voice in politics long before they all had the vote at the national level.

Nor was the national vote denied only to women. For instance, the right to vote depended on certain property and wealth qualifications. It was not a 'right of men', nor even a 'right of citizens'. It was not as if all women were excluded from a right that all men had. In 1884 and 1885, the vote was extended to agricultural workers for the first time. In fact, all men over 21 only gained the vote in 1918, when women over 30 were given the vote.

Expressed another way, this fact puts the struggles of suffragettes in context. That is: in 1918 all men and women were given the vote. The only inequality was that the voting age for men was 21 whereas the voting age for women was 30. Ten years later, this age disparity was eliminated, and the voting age made 21 for both sexes. It was hardly that women as a class suffered a terrible injustice in a way that men did not.

Another aspect of this struggle was that the House of Commons gained considerably in power during the nineteenth century, and so having the vote became much more significant than it had previously. We are used to thinking today that the lower house is the one with real, and representative, power; and so being able to vote for representatives is very important. That was not the case in nineteenth-century Britain. Only after 1872, when secret ballots were brought in, could workers actually vote freely without fear of reprisals from employer or landlord—if they were eligible to vote at all. This meant that public opinion began to have real force in parliament. The House of Lords was not legally reduced in power until 1911.[9]

The fight for women to have the vote was part of this development of representative government. As England was gaining in wealth, and the majority of people released from the grinding burden of poverty; as education was becoming more widely available and the taxes on newspapers and papers removed; as the House of Commons increased in number and power, the people of England began to demand a greater say in the running of their country. Some women had to wait a little longer than men for their rights to be recognized; but theirs was not the only, or necessarily the worst, struggle.

HELP FOR PROSTITUTES

We find a different kind of distortion of history concerning the legal victories that really were won by and for women. For instance, an important campaign was waged against the Contagious Diseases Act, from its introduction in 1870 until its eventual repeal in 1886. These Acts allowed for the compulsory medical examination of prostitutes. The specific argument rested mainly on the double standard of sexual morality which the Acts not only assumed, but enshrined; that the prostitutes were responsible for prostitution, while their customers were innocent. It ignored not only the extent to which prostitutes were the victims of male lust, but also the part played by low wages and poor employment opportunities in forcing girls into prostitution.

---

9. See David Thomas, *ibid.*, ch. 9.

The repeal of the Contagious Diseases Act is an example of something claimed as a feminist victory which was actually fought on grounds almost totally alien to modern feminism. Josephine Butler, who led the campaign, was a suffragist (campaigning for women's right to vote), who promoted education for girls and employment opportunities for women. She began campaigning against the law contained in the Contagious Diseases Act, protesting that it deprived the most defenceless class of its constitutional rights. Whereas the (all-male) parliament had regarded the prostitutes as entirely to blame both for their activity and the spread of disease, Butler and her fellow campaigners (both men and women) saw prostitution as sexual slavery. Prostitutes could not be regarded as outcasts simply because of the nature of their work. Indeed, the regulation system meant that women were doomed to staying in prostitution because, once stigmatized, they had no chance of finding alternative employment—and the stigma of examination could be visited on any woman who seemed suspicious, whether she actually was a prostitute or not.

> *I mention this incident merely as an illustration of the spirit of our women in their jealous guardianship of the sacredness of womanhood even in the persons of the most degraded of their sisters. I myself believe this spirit to be thoroughly in accord with that of our Master, Christ.*
>
> (JOSEPHINE BUTLER, 1888)

Butler and her colleagues also campaigned against the legislation because it sanctioned male 'vice'. A parliamentary report in 1871 had stated that while the prostitutes were transgressors using lust for gain, their customers were merely undertaking "an irregular indulgence of a natural impulse". That is, this law accepted and embodied male adultery. The activists' call was for a single standard of sexuality, the same standard that already applied to women (that is, sex within marriage only). Butler's campaign was very popular, and 'social purity' groups ('social purity' being a catch-cry of nineteenth-century women's activism) sprang up all over Britain.

Josephine Butler considered her movement a consciously Christian one, rooted in the will of God and preceded by prayer. She listed among her supporters a wide range of Protestant denominations, as well as Unitarians and Jews, although she had found it difficult to raise church support at the beginning of her campaign. Her own rather mystical views probably made it easier to accept any number of religious supporters, hoping merely that they accepted her drive for justice and compassion within a Christian framework.

Indeed, while modern feminism has been distinctly anti-Christian and in favour of redefining sexual morality, this was not at all the ideological tenor of nineteenth-century women's movements. While the tradition of equal-rights feminism had some influence, with its roots in the Enlightenment, a significant part of women's activism came from the evangelical movement. It did not argue from human rights, but on the need to give women's qualities more significance in public life. Early in the nineteenth century, a majority of those involved in activism had entered for overtly religious reasons; this declined over time, but still constituted around 35% of the identifiable female activists at the end of the century. Freethinkers, the secularists or atheists against religion, were never as large a group, and declined from a larger to a smaller minority over the century. In spite of modern claims that religion has been a major oppressor of women, many of the original women activists grounded their feminism in their religion.

Yet this attitude on the part of nineteenth-century women activists seems rather hard to stomach in modern feminist histories. It is apparently astonishing for some modern writers that

their claimed forebears were traditionally, conservatively religious—not only hard to believe, but rather shameful. Feminist
historian Barbara Caine comments on this tendency in feminist
thought when she admits it is "tempting to look for feminist her-
itages and influence only in radical and progressive quarters and
amongst those overtly protesting or rebelling against the oppression of women". She recognizes, however, that "it is impossible to
do so. For such an approach ignores the importance to feminists
of conservative women and of some conservative stereotypes of
femininity which they used effectively in making their arguments, demands, and claims".[10]

Feminism also claims for itself a strong tradition in America; and
recently, a comprehensive history of feminism in Australia has
also been written. There are similar histories for European countries and, increasingly, third-world countries. If the quality of
writing about British women's movements is anything to go by,
one begins to lose confidence in feminist scholarship. What distortions exist in the feminist histories of these other countries?[11]

---

10. Barbara Caine, *ibid.*, pp. 42-43.
11. For instance, early Australian feminists generally considered the family to be central to society and a woman's best goal marriage and motherhood, although demanding space for those women who wished to or had to remain single. Indeed, their
emphasis on the importance of motherhood was the basis for much of the argument
for women's rights.; it was their particular forte which could contribute to the better-
ment of society, providing the public world with influences that men could not give.
As Vida Goldstein (who founded the Woman's Federal Political Association and considered one of Australia's leading feminists) wrote in 1903, "It is suicidal to divorce the
home and the State...the State is only an aggregate of families, and as the best-governed
family is where husband and wife work together in the highest interest of their children, so the best-governed State will be that where men and women work together in
the highest interest of the people". Although modern feminists now decry some of their
achievements, the earlier wave of Australian feminism considered that the protection of
women as wives and mothers was their highest goal.

The myth of history

There have been many strong women who have fought for justice and compassion for those who needed it, against entrenched prejudice and legalized injustice, and who have won. These women deserve to have their stories told truly. Some may have been motivated by ideas which are similar to modern feminist ideology. However, many of those claimed by feminism were not so motivated, and would probably have been horrified to be included in the same tradition. There is not a long tradition of women fighting against male oppression, as told by modern feminism. There are women and men fighting against oppression in any manner of forms, and women and men resisting because they are the oppressors. Major social changes for women have resulted; so have major social changes for men, children, working-classes, racial minorities, the disabled, the sick and many other groups. We can be glad of the victories where justice and compassion have triumphed. We should not let the efforts of women who fought hard for these things be usurped by an ideology that was totally foreign to them.

⊨ *Chapter 6* ⊨

ONCE A FEMINIST

I began this book as a feminist, thinking that feminism was basically a reasonable position. I thought it was an admirable movement which had uncovered real injustice and had worked to correct it. I thought that, despite perhaps some mistakes of extremism, it was a movement we should celebrate and recognize, for surely feminism was a philosophy that is good for women and therefore good for society.

I have discovered that it is not. This has been hard to accept; it had to hit me in the face before I recognized it fully, for like others of my generation I have grown up living and breathing feminism. It seems simply natural and obvious that a woman can do anything she wants to, can have family, career, and anything else she likes. It was quite a shock to examine feminism and find that it evaporates under scrutiny.

Feminism cannot succeed in creating the equality and harmony between men and women it desires because it is based on falsehoods. Its individualism and freedom led it to attack the social structures that were good for women (marriage, family) and now women are suffering. It also led to a rights–based competition which leads to accelerating pain for both men and women. Its unyielding emphasis on personal autonomy, at virtually any cost, is destructive to all but the most powerful who end up alone at the top. It teaches an unreasoning morality that sacrifices the weak in the interests of the strong and will propagate falsehoods to shore up its irrational position.

Feminism has led us to decree that a woman must work to matter, to be a proper human being, whether she's single or not, whether a mother or not, and whether she wants to or not. The result is that now the stay-at-home mum is socially and financially disadvantaged; and the vast majority of working mothers and their children are also disadvantaged. Feminism has not been about creating opportunities for women, but prescribing morals to women—and its morals do not work. For all the rhetoric about women caring and being compassionate, feminism doesn't promote it. It encourages women to be as selfish as men. No wonder it is so popular—the freedom to be selfish and powerful is a sweet dream that dies hard.

> *"Nobody is ever an ex-feminist", says Robin Morgan. "Nobody ever says, 'Well, I was a feminist'... that's because freedom is contagious and it feels good to be capable, to be competent, to be your own woman."[1]*

Well, I was a feminist. I am now an ex-feminist, because I have discovered that it does not bring freedom, and if I want to be competent and empowered what I need is truth. Feminism has a glossy sheen of fine-sounding promises: freedom, independence, fulfilment, transcendence, happiness. But most of these it just can't deliver, and those it can are not the idyllic goals it claimed.

Feminism is a selfish movement, with no sustainable philosophy, a fabricated history, and an incoherent morality. It does not bring freedom and fulfilment for women, and it will not right injustices. Many of us in this world rightly feel anger and sorrow at the terrible lives women all over the world can face; poverty and starvation in some places, violence and abuse almost everywhere. The answer is not to become more selfish. That can only make injustice worse.

Facing this truth is hard, for this is an imperfect world and there will always be those willing to exploit women where they can. Justice will probably only be found in small pockets of the world for limited times, and we must do what we can to extend those places and times. We will only do that by resisting, not promoting, self-centredness. Only then, in a world that promotes injustice so well, can we hope to make some changes for the better.

---

1. *Saints and Divas, op. cit.,* p. 101.

⊰ *Epilogue* ⊱

CHRISTIANITY AND WOMEN

In one sense, it has been easy to shoot at feminism for, once looked at clearly, it is a large and slow-moving target. Nonetheless, I had been content to accept it until my research gave me reason to question previous assumptions, and to examine the evidence in more detail. I then realised that an alternative framework of thinking gives a much more satisfying view of women and their experience.

For feminism is not the only philosophy that has ever valued women, contrary to its own claims. Other life philosophies consider that women should be valued in their own right, as worthwhile and necessary human beings—and without insisting that women are only thus valuable if they act just like men (surely the deepest insult). The alternative that I realised makes much more sense of the data is biblical Christianity. This is a philosophy that has received considerable bad press from feminists, but little real consideration. For despite its reputation as an oppressor of women, what is taught in the Bible is that women, different from men, matter. It is a freedom from the tyranny of having to be the same as men in order to matter. If you have been brought up a feminist, it will probably be difficult to examine the Bible seriously, for you will have been taught to assume that it is anti-women. It is not. It is simply unfeminist. As we have seen, feminism itself can be profoundly anti-women. Christianity values women, but has a completely different worldview, one that is more attractive, and which works.

There is much more to be said on this topic; but being a believer in writing only one book at a time, in this epilogue I only point in the direction of a future book that needs to be written. Biblical Christianity presents a coherent, challenging and uplifting philosophy of women which may well be what many women attracted to feminism are actually looking for. For a start, it can explain precisely what went wrong with feminism. It suffers from the disease of self, which the Bible calls sin (contrary to the popular understanding that sin means sexual misdemeanour) whereby we discard everything to pursue freedom but find disaster and enslavement instead.

> *A wife of noble character who can find? She is worth far more than rubies. Her husband has full confidence in her and lacks nothing of value…she is clothed with strength and dignity; she can laugh at the days to come. She speaks with wisdom, and faithful instruction is on her tongue.*
>
> (PROVERBS 31:10-11, 25-26)

How much better is a worldview which promotes interdependence, not independence; building community over self-determination; the opportunity to serve others in community rather than a war for rights; and mutuality, not autonomy. This is a worldview which works for us as human beings, wanting to relate to others, and wanting a way in which to do it which will preserve the dignity and mutual respect of individuals.

Moreover, the Bible provides a point of reference whereby the endless and confusing question of 'what is a woman' can be satisfactorily solved. It provides the grounds for an answer in the God who created both men and women; it tells us that he designed humanity to be relational. Without romanticising the world, it presents examples of women secure in relationships with husband and children, and powerful in their dealings with the world. Their relationships work because they are part of a web of humanity, made by God to function well together in complementary, interconnecting lives.

It will take another book to explore the riches of this world-view, one which has been largely forgotten in our feminism-dominated era. I find the prospect exciting. I hope you do too.

⇥ *References* ⇤

I t is difficult to compile a reference list for a book such as this, not only because it has been influenced by many works which have ostensibly nothing to do with feminism, but also because even a list of the works about feminism can only look hopelessly incomplete given the libraries of feminist works available. In researching for this book, I have tried to read all the major and many of the minor books in the feminist body of work, as well as various other works relevant to the topic. No doubt there are omissions. Listed here are those works (books only) for which I had recorded the details and which seemed most relevant. I have not included the numbers of newspaper articles, book reviews, academic papers and magazines which now fill my files.

Alcorn, R.C., *Pro Life Answers to Pro Choice Arguments*. 1992, Portland, Oregon: Multnomah Books.

Anderson, G., *Fixation of Wages in Australia*. 1st ed. 1929, Melbourne: Melbourne University Press.

Arndt, B., *Private Lives*. 1986, Ringwood: Penguin Books Australia.

Banks, O., *Becoming a Feminist: The Social Origins of 'First Wave' Feminism*. 1986, Brighton: Wheatsheaf Books.

Beasley, C., *What is Feminism, Anyway? Understanding Contemporary Feminist Thought*. 1999, Sydney: Allen & Unwin.

De Beauvoir, S., *The Prime of Life*. 1962, Harmondsworth: Penguin Books.

De Beauvoir, S., *Memoirs of a Dutiful Daughter*. 1963, Harmondsworth: Penguin Books.

De Beauvoir, S., *The Second Sex*. 1972, Harmondsworth: Penguin Books.

Black, C., (ed). *Married Women's Work: Being the Report of an Enquiry Undertaken by the Women's Industrial Council*. Virago edition offset from the first edition published in 1915 by G. Bell, London. 1983, Virago: London.

Caine, B., *English Feminism 1780-1980*. 1997, Oxford: Oxford University Press.

Chadwick, O., *The Victorian Church*. 1970, London: Adam and Charles Black.

Chan, C., *Divorce—an Australian Woman's Guide*. 1983, Melbourne: William Heinemann Australia.

Comer, L., *Wedlocked Women*. 1974, Leeds: Feminist Books.

Cook, M., *Just Wages: History of the Campaign for Pay Equity 1984-1993*. 1994, Wellington: Coalition for Equal Value Equal Pay (CEVEP)

Coward, R., *Sacred Cows: Is Feminism Relevant to the New Millennium?* 1999, London: HarperCollins Publishers.

Curthoys, A., S. Eade, and P. Spearritt, (eds). *Women at Work*. 1975, Australian Society for the Study of Labour History: Canberra.

Curthoys, J., *Feminist Amnesia: The Wake of Women's Liberation*. 1997, London and New York: Routledge.

Davis, E.G., *The First Sex*. 1971, Baltimore: Penguin Books.

Department of Employment and Industrial Relations: Women's Bureau, *Women and Existing Retirement Income Systems: Submission to the Senate Standing Committee on Social Welfare*. 1985, Canberra: Australian Government Publishing Service.

Eagleton, M., (ed). *Feminist Literary Theory: A Reader*. 1986,

Blackwell Publishers: Cambridge, Massachusetts.

Estés, C.P., *Women Who Run With the Wolves: Contacting the Power of the Wild Woman*. 1992, London: Rider.

Evans, M., (ed). *The Woman Question: Readings on the Subordination of Women*. 1982, Fontana Paperbacks: London.

Faludi, S., *Backlash: The Undeclared War against Women*. 1991 and 1992, London: Chatto & Windus.

Faludi, S., *Stiffed: The Betrayal of the Modern Man*. 1999, London: Chatto & Windus. Fisher, H., *The First Sex: The Natural Talents of Women and How they are Changing the World*. 1999, Sydney: Random House Australia.

Forster, C., *Wages and Wage Policy: Australia in the Depression 1929-34*. Working Papers in Economic History. 1988, Canberra: The Australian National University.

Frasse, G. and M. Perrot, (eds). *A History of Women in the West. Volume 4: Emerging Feminism from Revolution to World War*. 1993, The Belknap Press of Harvard University Press: Cambridge, Massachusetts and London, England.

French, M., *The War Against Women*. 1992, London: Penguin Books.

Friedan, B., *The Feminine Mystique*. 1963, London: Penguin Books.

Friedan, B., *Life So Far*. 2000, New York: Simon & Schuster.

Funder, K., *Remaking Families: Adaptation of Parents and Children to Divorce*. 1996, Melbourne: Australian Institute of Family Studies.

Garner, H. *The First Stone: Some Questions about Sex and Power*. 1995, Sydney: Picador.

Greer, G., *The Female Eunuch*. 1970, London: Paladin.

Greer, G., *The Whole Woman*. 1999, New York: Alfred A. Knopf.

Gregory, R.G., A. Daly, and V. Ho, *A Tale of Two Countries: Equal Pay for Women in Australia and Britain*. 1986, Canberra: The Centre for Economic Policy Research.

Grillet, S., *Feminism for Teenagers*. 1997, London: Picadilly Press.

House of Representatives Standing Committee on Legal and Constitutional Affairs, *To Have and to Hold: a report of the inquiry into aspects of family services*, 1998, Canberra.

Harper, J. and L. Richards, *Mothers and Working Mothers*. 1979, Harmondsworth: Penguin Books.

Hutchinson, E.J., *Women's Wages: A Study of the Wages of Industrial Women and Measures Suggested to Increase Them*. reprinted 1968, New York: Columbia University Press, AMS Press Inc.

Hutson, J., *Six Wage Concepts*. 1971, Sydney: Amalgamated Engineering Union.

Jong, E., *How to Save Your Own Life*. 1978, London: Granada Publishing.

Kelly, S., *The Prize and the Price: The Changing World of Women who Return to Study*. 1987, Sydney: Methuen Haynes.

Kemp, S. and J. Squires, (eds). *Feminisms*. 1997, Oxford University Press: Oxford.

Lake, M., *Getting Equal: The History of Australian Feminism*. 1999, Sydney: Allen and Unwin.

Levine, P., *Victorian Feminism 1850-1900*. 1987, London: Hutchinson.

Lyndon, N., *No More Sex War*. 1992, London: Mandarin.

Maushart, S., *The Mask of Motherhood: How Mothering Changes Everything and Why we Pretend It Doesn't*. 1997, Sydney: Random House Australia.

Mead, M., *Male and Female: A Study of the Sexes in a Changing World*. 1950, London: Victor Gollancz Ltd.

Mercer, J., (ed). *The Other Half: Women in Australian Society*. 1975, Penguin Books: Harmondsworth.

Miller, C. and K. Smith, *Words and Women: New Language in New Times*. 1976, Harmondsworth: Penguin Books.

Miller, J.B., *Toward a New Psychology of Women*. 1976, Harmondsworth: Penguin Books.

Mitchell, J., *Woman's Estate*. 1971, Harmondsworth: Penguin Books.

Mitchell, J., *Psychoanalysis and Feminism*. 1974, Harmondsworth: Penguin Books. Mitchell, J. and A. Oakley, (eds). *The Rights and Wrongs of Women*. 1976, Penguin Books: Harmondsworth.

Mitchell, S., *Icons, Saints & Divas: Intimate Conversations with Women who Changed the World*. 1997, Sydney: HarperCollins Publishers.

Morgan, R., (ed). *Sisterhood is Powerful: An Anthology of Writings from the Women's Liberation Movement*. 1970, Vintage Books: New York.

Ochiltree, G., *Effects of Child Care on Young Children*. 1994, Melbourne: Australian Institute of Family Studies.

Ochiltree, G. and D. Edgar, *Today's Child Care, Tomorrow's Children*. 1995, Melbourne: Australian Institute of Family Studies.

Office of Manpower Economics, *Equal Pay: First Report by the Office of Manpower Economics*. 1972, London: Her Majesty's Stationery Office.

Owen, M. and S. Shaw, (eds). *Working Women: Discussion Papers from the Working Women's Centre, Melbourne*. 1979, Sisters Publishing Ltd: Melbourne.

Patterson, P. and M. Armstrong, *An Employer's Guide to Equal Pay*. 1972, London: Kogan Page (Associates).

Payne, T. and P.D. Jensen, *Pure Sex*. 1998, Sydney: Matthias Media.

Pettman, B.O., (ed). *Equal Pay for Women: Progress and Problems in Seven Countries*. 1975, MCB Books in association with the International Institute of Social Economics: Bradford, West Yorkshire.

Phillips, M., *The Sex-Change Society: Feminised Britain and the Neutered Male*. 1999, London: The Social Market Foundation.

Reist, M.T., *Giving Sorrow Words: Women's Stories of Grief After Abortion*. 2000, Sydney: Duffy & Snellgrove.

Roiphe, K., *The Morning After*. 1993, London: Hamish Hamilton.

Rowbotham, S., *Woman's Consciousness, Man's World*. 1973, Harmondsworth: Penguin Books.

Rowbotham, S., *Hidden from History: 300 Years of Women's Oppression and the Fight Against It*. 1974, Ringwood: Penguin Books Australia.

Sommers, C.H., *Who Stole Feminism? How Women Have Betrayed Women*. 1994, New York and others: Simon & Schuster.

Summers, A., *Damned Whores and God's Police*. 1975, Ringwood: Penguin Books Australia.

Thomas, D., *England in the Nineteenth Century: 1815-1914*. 1950, Harmondsworth: Penguin Books.

Thomas, D., *Not Guilty: Men: The Case for the Defence*. 1993, London: Weidenfeld & Nicolson.

Tomaselli, S., (ed). *Mary Wollstonecroft: A Vindication of the Rights of Men with A Vindication of the Rights of Woman and Hints*. 1995, Cambridge University Press: Cambridge.

Trevelyan, G.M., *British History in the Nineteenth Century and After (1782-1919)*. 1965, Harmondsworth: Penguin Books.

Union of Australian Women, *Women and Wages in the War Years 1940-1945*, n.d.

Walter, N., (ed). *On the Move: Feminism for a New Generation*. 1999, Virago Press: London.

Wandersee, W.D., *Women's Work and Family Values 1920-1940*. 1981, Cambridge Massachusetts and London England: Harvard University Press.

Wandor, M., *Once a Feminist: Stories of a Generation*. 1990, London: Virago.

Wolcott, I and Glezer, H., *Work and Family Life: Achieving Integration*. 1995, Melbourne: Australian Institute of Family Studies.

Wolf, N., *The Beauty Myth: How Images of Beauty are Used Against Women*. 1990, London: Vintage.

Wolf, N., *Fire with Fire: The New Female Power and How It Will Change the 21st Century*. 1993, London: Chatto & Windus.

Wolf, N., *Promiscuities: A Secret History of Female Desire*. 1997, London: Chatto & Windus.

Zola, N. and R. Singer, *True Stories from the Land of Divorce*. 1995, Sydney: Pan Macmillan Australia.

Other Matthias Media resources
from the same author...

The essence of
the Reformation

Corruption in the church. Political turmoil and intrigue. A clash of new ideas and ancient pagan religions. Courageous and extraordinary individuals. Doctrinal disputes that were matters of life and death.

These things and more make up what is often called the 'Reformation', that tumultuous period of European history ranging from around 1517 to the turn of the century. Unfortunately, the events, people and ideas are generally not well known today, even though in many ways, the Reformation made our modern world what it is. It provided the thinking and beliefs that shaped intellectual and religious endeavour for centuries to come, down to the present day.

In this short book, Kirsten Birkett brings us the essence of the Reformation—the social and religious soil in which it grew, the events and people which shaped it, the ideas and doctrines for which many of them died.

ORDERING DETAILS:

Australia

Matthias Media
Telephone: +61-2-9663 1478
Facsimile: +61 2-9662 4289
Email: sales@matthiasmedia.com.au

United Kingdom

The Good Book Company
Telephone: +20-8942 0880
Facsimile: +20-8942-0990
Email: admin@thegoodbook.co.uk

www.matthiasmedia.com.au

The essence
of Psychology

As the new millennium dawns, the psychologist has replaced the clergyman as the dispenser of wisdom and peace in our confused and troubled world. When we are depressed or anxious or our marriages are in trouble, it is to psychology that we routinely turn for insight and therapy. It is hard to believe that psychology hardly existed a century ago, and that its prominent place in modern life has only come about in the last generation.

In this short book, Dr Kirsten Birkett offers a concise and readable summary of the essence of psychology—what it is, how it came about, and how it relates to the Christian worldview of the Bible. Dr Birkett examines the various kinds of psychological therapies, and how these are based on different views of how the mind works. She also scrutinizes the deeper assumptions of psychology, and asks how a Christian view of humanity and the mind relates to mental illness.

This penetrating analysis of the insights and claims of psychology makes for fascinating reading. It will be of particular benefit to those who struggle with their own mental health, as well as those who support them.

ORDERING DETAILS:

Australia

Matthias Media
Telephone: +61-2-9663 1478
Facsimile: +61 2-9662 4289
Email: sales@matthiasmedia.com.au

United Kingdom

The Good Book Company
Telephone: +20-8942 0880
Facsimile: +20-8942-0990
Email: admin@thegoodbook.co.uk

www.matthiasmedia.com.au

Classics of the Reformation

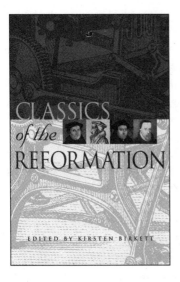

The Reformation gave rise to some classic works of Christian literature, many of which still are without equal in expressing the truth of the Bible.

This collection contains four such works (previously published separately as Matthias Pocket Classics): Martin Luther on 'The Freedom of the Christian', John Calvin on 'Prayer', William Tyndale on 'A Pathway into Scripture', and Thomas Cranmer on 'Saving Faith'.

Gain a taste of the riches of our Reformation heritage in this easy-to-read anthology.

(Edited by Kirsten Birkett)

ORDERING DETAILS:

Australia

Matthias Media
Telephone: +61-2-9663 1478
Facsimile: +61 2-9662 4289
Email: sales@matthiasmedia.com.au

United Kingdom

The Good Book Company
Telephone: +20-8942 0880
Facsimile: +20-8942-0990
Email: admin@thegoodbook.co.uk

www.matthiasmedia.com.au

Unnatural Enemies

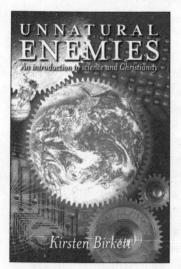

AN INTRODUCTION TO
SCIENCE AND CHRISTIANITY

"History records that whenever science and orthodoxy have been fairly opposed, the latter has been forced to retire from the lists, bleeding and crushed, if not annihilated; scotched if not slain." So argued Thomas Huxley, one of the nineteenth century's great champions of science against Christian belief.

Was he right? Are science and Christianity destined to be bitter enemies? Is it possible to be a Christian and a good scientist?

In this compellingly readable introduction to the subject, Kirsten Birkett looks at both science and Christianity, clearly explaining what both are about, and dispelling many common confusions and misunderstandings. She argues that while there are no necessary grounds for the two to be at war, there is still reason to think that the conflict might continue.

For all devotees of science—Christian or non-Christian, professional, student or lay—Dr Birkett's perspective as both a Christian and an historian of science sheds new light on these perennial questions.

ORDERING DETAILS:

Australia

Matthias Media
Telephone: +61-2-9663 1478
Facsimile: +61 2-9662 4289
Email: sales@matthiasmedia.com.au

United Kingdom

The Good Book Company
Telephone: +20-8942 0880
Facsimile: +20-8942-0990
Email: admin@thegoodbook.co.uk

www.matthiasmedia.com.au